The Bible says, "One who has unreliable friends soon comes to ruin, but there is a friend who sticks closer than a brother." God designed us for relationship, and it is to friendship we are called. In our world, rugged individualism and resilient independence are admired, but this path leads to loneliness and despair. Justin Whitmel Earley's *Made for People* is a clarion call to covenant friendship—a deep, abiding love that comes from vulnerability and trust. Don't go to ruin; be encouraged and equipped as you read—and pursue friendship.

—KYLE IDLEMAN, senior pastor, Southeast Christian Church; bestselling author, *When Your Way Isn't Working*

Few of us want to admit how lonely we are. It feels shameful, even though almost everyone is facing loneliness right now. In this book, Justin Whitmel Earley draws us out of all of that to show us not just why we need people but how to combat this lonely age. This book is practical and timely and will make you feel less alone.

—RUSSELL MOORE, editor-in-chief, *Christianity Today*

Justin's exploration of the art of covenant friendship in this book will both convict and encourage you toward becoming more and more like Christ.

—RUTH CHOU SIMONS, *Wall Street Journal* bestselling author; artist; founder, gracelaced.com

In an age when loneliness and isolation feel especially pernicious, we desperately need steady wisdom and clear guidance toward a better way. In *Made for People*, Justin Whitmel Earley offers us just that. Earley is a wise, compelling, and gentle guide, helping readers better understand and cultivate the God-given gift of friendship. I'm grateful for this book and am confident it will bless its readers.

—CLAUDE ATCHO, pastor, Church of the Resurrection, Charlottesville, Virginia; author, *Reading Black Books: How African American Literature Can* ’

T0054535

In my experience, the men who are experiencing the deepest pain are often the men who are most alone. This book won't just bring hope, it will point you to Jesus and, as a result, bring healing.

—**JERRAD LOPES**, founder, Dad Tired

I don't know about you, but it can feel like an admission of inadequacy to confess that I have fewer intimate friendships than I would like. Worse, it can feel like this is an indictment of who I am as a person, an intractable, interminable problem with no solution and no path forward. Thankfully, Justin Whitmel Earley provides a path forward and helps us to see, to paraphrase Dallas Willard, that friendship is opposed not to effort but to earning. I learned so much from this book and have found it to be helpful in my own life. I especially appreciate Justin's focus on spiritual disciplines and the centrality of prayer in friendship. Let this book guide you to a life of friendship.

—**MICHAEL WEAR**, author, *The Spirit of Our Politics: Spiritual Formation and the Renovation of Public Life*

For relationship, we were created. God conceived us for himself and each other. So why do we often try to go it alone; why do we think we can live on our own? In this new book, *Made for People*, Justin Whitmel Earley implores us to exercise the art and habit of fostering life-giving friendship. Through principles and practices, you will be challenged and equipped to cultivate friendships that go the distance—something simple, yet not easy.

—**JONATHAN "JP" POKLUDA**, lead pastor, Harris Creek Baptist Church; bestselling author, *Why Do I Do What I Don't Want to Do?*; host, *Becoming Something* podcast

MADE
FOR
PEOPLE

UD-25-29-2003-1008

JUSTIN
WHITMEL EARLEY

MADE FOR PEOPLE

WHY WE DRIFT INTO
LONELINESS AND HOW
TO FIGHT FOR A LIFE
OF **FRIENDSHIP**

ZONDERVAN
BOOKS

ZONDERVAN BOOKS

Made for People
Copyright © 2023 by Avodah, LLC

Requests for information should be addressed to:
Zondervan, *3900 Sparks Dr. SE, Grand Rapids, Michigan 49546*

Zondervan titles may be purchased in bulk for educational, business, fundraising, or sales promotional use. For information, please email SpecialMarkets@Zondervan.com.

ISBN 978-0-310-36300-2 (softcover)
ISBN 978-0-310-36304-0 (audio)
ISBN 978-0-310-36302-6 (ebook)

All Scripture quotations, unless otherwise indicated, are taken from The Holy Bible, New International Version®, NIV®. Copyright © 1973, 1978, 1984, 2011 by Biblica, Inc.® Used by permission of Zondervan. All rights reserved worldwide. www.Zondervan.com. The "NIV" and "New International Version" are trademarks registered in the United States Patent and Trademark Office by Biblica, Inc.®

Scripture quotations marked ESV are taken from the ESV® Bible (The Holy Bible, English Standard Version®). Copyright © 2001 by Crossway, a publishing ministry of Good News Publishers. Used by permission. All rights reserved.

Scripture quotations marked ISV are from the International Standard Version. Copyright © 1995–2014 by ISV Foundation. All rights reserved internationally. Used by permission of Davidson Press, LLC.

Scripture quoted by permission. Quotations designated (NET©) are from the NET Bible® copyright ©1996–2017 by Biblical Studies Press, L.L.C. http://netbible.com. All rights reserved.

Scripture quotations marked NLT are taken from the Holy Bible, New Living Translation. © 1996, 2004, 2015 by Tyndale House Foundation. Used by permission of Tyndale House Publishers, Inc., Carol Stream, Illinois 60188. All rights reserved.

Any internet addresses (websites, blogs, etc.) and telephone numbers in this book are offered as a resource. They are not intended in any way to be or imply an endorsement by Zondervan, nor does Zondervan vouch for the content of these sites and numbers for the life of this book.

All rights reserved. No part of this publication may be reproduced, stored in a retrieval system, or transmitted in any form or by any means—electronic, mechanical, photocopy, recording, or any other—except for brief quotations in printed reviews, without the prior permission of the publisher.

Published in association with Don Gates of the literary agency The Gates Group, www.the-gates-group.com.

Cover design: Micah Kandros
Cover illustrations: Franzi / Shutterstock
Interior art: Sarah Shaw
Interior design: Denise Froehlich

Printed in the United States of America

23 24 25 26 27 LBC 5 4 3 2 1

For The Cast
With so much gratitude for teaching me
the arts and habits of covenant friendship

WHENEVER YOU GO OUT, WALK TOGETHER, AND WHEN YOU REACH YOUR DESTINATION, STAY TOGETHER.

—Rule of St. Augustine, chapter IV

Contents

Introduction

You Were Made for People

Most life-changing moments are, at first, completely unremarkable.

It was true for me. The moment that forever changed my life passed rather quickly.

I remember Steve and I were standing beside a locker. I remember that I was in tenth grade. That's about it for the details I recall clearly.

On the contrary, I remember the details of the year before very clearly. Because they were made so excruciatingly memorable by the pain of loneliness.

My dad had been elected to state office. The attorney general of Virginia, in fact. So before ninth grade my family moved to Richmond, and I was known in theory—as the new politician's kid—but unknown as a real person. Everyone else seemed to have neighbors and friendships and clubs. I knew no one.

What's worse, I was a complete nerd. I still—I kid you not—tucked in my shirt. I played the clarinet. I had some Bible verses on the front of my binder, too, 'cause that helped.

In my spare time I tried to teach myself the drums and begged my parents to let me quit the clarinet section. I also spent time practicing skateboarding and hacky sack, both things I saw cooler kids doing, and I assumed they were, perhaps, entry points to the unknown social world.

My entire ninth-grade year was a wasteland of loneliness, which meant that every decision—from what color shirt to wear (most of mine still had collars) to whether to answer a question in class (I was slowly learning that getting them all right was not winning me points)—was a cause of great anxiety.

I only now see that this is how just about everyone feels when we live alone.

Without someone else to affirm our existence in the world, we stumble along unsure of everything, doubting the biggest and smallest decisions alike. What we usually don't realize is that all that fear and anxiety is not the product of facing difficult circumstances, it is the product of facing those circumstances alone.

Which is why everything changed in the fall of tenth grade, after that conversation at the lockers with Steve.

Steve and I had met at a youth retreat a few weeks before. When my parents dropped me off at the retreat center, I knew no one there. I remember sitting in a large cafeteria alone, wondering what I was going to do all weekend.

Besides that, I remember only wandering outside and finding my way across the retreat center to a skateboard half pipe where some kids were trying to drop in. Lucky me, I had been practicing. I asked if I could have a turn. I borrowed the skateboard Steve was using, dropped in successfully, skated a moment or two, and people clapped.

It's a haze now, but it may have been the best experience of my life up to that point.

I started talking to Steve, and we skated the pipe for a while, and then—by some new social permission—I was given access to walk around with him and his friends. We found a drum set in the youth hall. Again, I had been practicing, what luck! Then we played hacky sack.

Never mind if you know nothing of the late-nineties culture

of skateboards or drums or hacky sack. Not many of my contemporaries did either. Which is why finding others who were interested meant so much to me—I thought I was the only one!

This series of moments was for me what C. S. Lewis famously describes as the beginning of friendship. The "You too?" moment. "Friendship arises [when two] companions discover that they have in common some insight or interest or even taste which . . . till that moment, each believed to be his own unique treasure (or burden). The typical expression of opening Friendship would be something like, 'What? You too? I thought I was the only one.' . . . It is when two such persons discover one another, when, whether with immense difficulties and semi-articulate fumblings . . . they share their vision—it is then that Friendship is born. And instantly they stand together in an immense solitude."[1]

"Semi-articulate fumblings" is such a delightful phrase that perfectly captures the beginnings of so many friendships. Especially mine.

So let me get back to the conversation that changed the rest of my life:

Standing at that locker, a few weeks after the youth retreat, one of us said, "Should we be best friends?"

Yes, it was that awkward.

I can't remember who asked the question, but it was probably Steve because he was comfortable saying whatever came to mind. (He still is.)

But the question was asked, and as if it were just a decision about where to go for lunch, both of us agreed that it was a good idea.

1. C. S. Lewis, "Friendship," in *The Four Loves* (San Francisco: HarperOne, 2017), 83.

That's it. End of memory. It was a conversation remarkable only for its weirdness and unmemorable for anyone but me.

That's what the beginning of friendship usually looks like. Two people fumbling to find something they deeply long for, can't quite name, and even if they could, would usually be too embarrassed to ask for.

Picture two boys messing around with a pack of matches. Now picture their faces when one of them successfully pops a spark and a fire begins to grow. The childish amazement, joy, and surprise all at once.

That was us. We were fumbling with some words. But we had no idea of their power or the fire that would follow.

As it turns out, words change things. We made a pact of friendship, and soon we found the "immense solitude" Lewis wrote of.

Our lives would never be the same. And ever since, I've had the uncanny feeling that I was made for friendship.

Created for People

I often think about the beginning of the world.

You may think that's a bit strange, but I think you should try it. It goes like this:

One day God is being quintessential God, making things from nothing, and he's doing it with his covenant friends—the Son and the Holy Spirit.

To imagine it right, you have got to see that they all think this whole creation thing is a spectacularly grand idea. It won't be without hiccups, they know, but they are providentially confident it will turn out to be a smashing success.

Picture it all for a moment: What it looks like for light to separate from darkness for the first time. The crash of an unfathomably large number of cubic gallons of water sloshing against the seabed. I wonder whether God the Son gets down on his knees and traces the shorelines carefully, the way a child concentrates on a drawing, while God the Father watches happily from behind the galaxy. Or whether both just laugh as the Holy Spirit splashes cosmic buckets of salt water on the earth to see where it falls, the way visual artist Makoto Fujimura seems to combine accident and purpose while flicking paint over a canvas to see the direction it runs.

I could go on, and I encourage you to do the same.

Think about what it sounds like to hear "Good!" ring out the first time over Himalayan mountain ranges. I imagine it sounds something like a dad's hearty laugh as he watches his kids play happily together in the back yard on a summer evening when, just for a moment, the world seems as it should be. Think about a peacock strutting for the first time or a lioness exploring her tail the way cats do. All for the first time and hearing the benediction thunder like a divine drum over all things, the Trinity—likely in three-part harmony—shouting, "Good! Good! Good!"

So there you have it. The beginning of the world.

Now I'm a corporate lawyer. Much more nerdy, not less, than the ninety-eight-pound, clarinet-playing freshman that I was. I write and negotiate contracts for a living. So imagining the beginning of the world as a wild, Trinitarian bash is a bit of a stretch for me too.[2] But it helps remind us of a key point: the beginning chapters of Genesis are a kind of poetry in Hebrew.

2. "It is, I grant you, a crass analogy; but crass analogies are the safest. . . . Accordingly, I give you the central truth that creation is the result of a Trinitarian bash" (Roger

Genesis may be true poetry, but it's still poetry. And in poetry, the writer picks every single word on purpose.

Note that God says "Good!" seven times in the beginning of Genesis. It's the rhythmic refrain of the chapter.

But that refrain gets halted with something like a record scratch as the music stops when we get to verse 18 of chapter 2: "The Lord God said, 'It is *not good* for the man to be alone.'"[3]

Not good!?

This, in the poetry, stands out like an inkblot on a white page. Everything halts like a paragraph left off midsentence. If the Bible is God's Word, you have to believe he does that on purpose. Why?

To stop you in your tracks and make you listen.

So hear it again because it could be the most important thing that God has ever said to you: "It is not good that you are alone."

Friendship Will Make or Break Your Life

In 2016 and 2017, sociologists started noticing Americans were dying younger and had been for a year or two.[4]

I'm sure it didn't happen quite like this, but I like to imagine a lead sociologist in a lab coat. He's walking around a brightly lit lab, ready to pack it in and head home for dinner, but he has to do his daily check on the Average American Life Expectancy Meter. So he walks over, clipboard in hand, takes a look, and frowns.

Farrar Capon, *The Romance of the Word: One Man's Love Affair with Theology* [Grand Rapids: Eerdmans, 1996], 177). See Capon's book for more on picturing this unconventional but theologically accurate understanding of the friendship that brought the world into being.

3. Genesis 2:18 (ESV), emphasis added.

4. "U.S. Life Expectancy 1950–2023," Macrotrends, accessed January 2023, www.macrotrends.net/countries/USA/united-states/life-expectancy.

He steps back, removes his glasses, and squints at the meter. It's pointing in the wrong direction.

He mutters something and gets his assistant, and they frown at it together. They finally agree that it is indeed true, the Average American Life Expectancy Meter is pointing backward. And it is not broken.

Sociologists didn't know it at the time, but something else was broken: the American soul. This marked the beginning of a multiyear decline.[5] It was the first time since the 1960s that we've seen such a drop. And in the 1960s the reason was clear: there was a flu epidemic. Just enough to bring the average life span down for two years. But in 2017, there was nothing like that in sight.

Our sociologists in lab coats here may be fictional, but this data is not.[6] Researchers found that the life expectancy was falling not because of a pandemic or cancer or anything else you might expect. The real reasons were grim and much more preventable stuff: young suicides, drug overdoses, alcoholism, and other preventable diseases of self-inflicted unhealth. In other words, "deaths of despair," a phrase that has now entered the American vocabulary.[7]

5. "'The latest CDC data show that the U.S. life expectancy has declined over the past few years,' said CDC Director Robert Redfield, M.D., in a Nov. 29 statement. 'Tragically, this troubling trend is largely driven by deaths from drug overdose and suicide.'" (Michael Devitt, "CDC Data Show U.S. Life Expectancy Continues to Decline," American Academy of Family Physicians, December 10, 2018, www.aafp .org/news/health-of-the-public/20181210lifeexpectdrop.html.)
6. See Ben Sasse, "Our Loneliness Epidemic," chap. 1 in *Them: Why We Hate Each Other—and How to Heal* (New York: St. Martin's Press, 2018).
7. "The phrase 'deaths of despair' has entered the nation's vocabulary the past few years to denote the rise of mortality among a subset of working-class whites from suicide, drugs, and alcohol. Its declining life expectancy is one of the most stunning trends in American life. The at-risk population tends to be unmarried, disconnected from civil society, marginally employed, and largely on their own." (Rich Lowry,

Why? Because friendship will make or break your life.

Around that time, studies showing that chronic loneliness is more dangerous to your health than smoking fifteen cigarettes a day began to get significant attention.[8] Experts called it an epidemic of loneliness,[9] because it's not the body that's killing us, it's the lonely soul that's killing the body.[10]

This epidemic of loneliness is not past tense.

The COVID-19 related deaths have only made it drastically worse. Statistics continue to be released that show a steady increase in our loneliness and a steady decline in our ability to stay alive. Data shows that through 2020 and 2021—between the epidemic of loneliness and the pandemic—Americans experienced the worst drop in life expectancy we have seen in a century.[11]

These statistics point to the enduring truth of God's words in Genesis: "It is not good for you to be alone."

"America Has a Loser Problem," *National Review*, October 30, 2018, www.nationalreview.com/2018/10/cesar-sayoc-robert-bowers-nikolas-cruz-marginal-isolated/.)

8. Julianne Holt-Lunstad, Timothy B. Smith, and J. Bradley Layton, "Social Relationships and Mortality Risk: A Meta-analytic Review," *PLOS Medicine* 7, no. 7 (2010): doi.org/10.1371/journal.pmed.1000316.

9. "America is suffering an epidemic of loneliness." (Arthur C. Brooks, "How Loneliness Is Tearing America Apart," *New York Times*, November 23, 2018, www.nytimes.com/2018/11/23/opinion/loneliness-political-polarization.html.)

10. It is interesting to watch researchers become more comfortable with prescribing intangible solutions to tangible health problems: "When you feel lonely you mainly need vitamin S, social relations. 'So you can share your feelings with someone you trust';" "Humans need others to survive. Social connection is crucial to human development, health, and survival." ("True: 'Long-Term Loneliness Is as Damaging to Your Health as Smoking 15 Cigarettes a Day,'" EU Fact Check, April 27, 2020, eufactcheck.eu/factcheck/true-long-term-loneliness-is-as-damaging-to-your-health-as-smoking-15-cigarettes-a-day/.)

11. "The average life expectancy of Americans fell precipitously in 2020 and 2021, the sharpest two-year decline in nearly 100 years." (Roni Caryn Rabin, "U.S. Life Expectancy Falls Again in 'Historic' Setback," *New York Times*, August 31, 2022, www.nytimes.com/2022/08/31/health/life-expectancy-covid-pandemic.html.)

Redefining Loneliness

But what does it mean to be alone?

If you are like me, you may bristle at the word *loneliness*. It can carry a sense of judgment, like a sickness we don't want to get caught having.

What I mean by loneliness is this: the feeling of being a person who used to have friends.

This loneliness is a universal struggle. It is a spiritual and physical reality that every single person will grapple with at multiple points in their life. It is not exactly the picture of a kid on the other end of the playground kicking rocks while all the cool kids do something fun. Many of us have experienced being an outcast, but that's only one version of loneliness. There are many, and they do not all look the same:

WHAT I MEAN BY LONELINESS IS THIS: THE FEELING OF BEING A PERSON WHO USED TO HAVE FRIENDS.

Loneliness comes from losing a loved one. Loneliness comes from moving away. It comes from changing churches or seeing a small group dissolve. Loneliness comes from being excluded or breaking up. It comes from divorce or being hurt by someone. But often, strangely, it also comes when you're surrounded by everyone but don't feel known by anyone.

Loneliness is the ache for something you used to have. Often an ache you cannot even name. As if relationship drifted away silently during the night, and you woke up in a world you cannot explain.

While loneliness comes in multiple forms, the commonality

is this: it is a sickness you cannot see.[12] Which is what makes it so dangerous. Most of us who are wrestling with loneliness wouldn't be able to diagnose it, and it is always the undiagnosed illnesses that wreak the worst havoc.

Consider whether this kind of loneliness may be present in your life right now.

Your loneliness might come from the paradox where you have a strong community in theory but do not have time for them in practice. Your loneliness might happen when you have incredible friends who have now moved away. Your loneliness could be the pain of not being understood by your family. Or perhaps it is the isolation you feel when you are going through something incredibly difficult and, though you're surrounded by friends, no one seems to understand it.

Note that these versions of loneliness all happen around people. That is the kind of loneliness I will be talking about in this book—the hidden pain of being surrounded by people but known by none of them.

If you feel any of this, you are not just normal, you are in the overwhelming majority. The current of modern life means that unless we swim with all of our might in the other direction, we will drift toward being someone who used to have friends.

This is the new normal of modern life. We are the most

---

12. During a conversation with Surgeon General of the United States Dr. Vivek H. Murthy discussing loneliness as America's number-one health problem, Arthur C. Brooks noted that you cannot tell from the outside whether someone is experiencing loneliness. "Loneliness can be a hidden phenomenon like many other areas of psychological difficulty or even mental illness—you can't tell. Sometimes you can't tell who is struggling with alcohol abuse, for example." (Rebecca Rashid and Arthur C. Brooks, "How to Know You're Lonely," *Atlantic*, October 12, 2021, www.theatlantic.com /podcasts/archive/2021/10/howto-friendship-loneliness-arthurbrooks-vivekmurthy -happiness/620281/.)

physically connected and yet spiritually isolated people who have ever walked the planet. Our default perspective should now be to assume that if you're a modern American, you are lonely.[13]

This is a spiritual crisis, not just a social one. Because this endemic modern loneliness is much more about your soul being hidden than it is about your body being hidden. And as it turns out, it is not just unpleasant, it is deadly.

Loneliness kills us body *and* soul. Because it's the opposite of what we were made for.

When the Truth Sounds Blasphemous

The wonderful thing about realizing you are made for people is that it explains why you feel the way you do.

This is why you feel like the world is so right when you have friends.[14] Because something *is* deeply right when that happens. This is why you also feel like the world is so wrong when friendships are gone or strained or broken. Because if relationships are not right, the world *is* wrong.

---

13. "If you look at the numbers around loneliness and you realize that you've got more people who are struggling with loneliness than have diabetes in this country—it made me realize I should probably change my default a little bit in terms of how I approach other people. Rather than assuming that people are connected and great and fine, I should probably recognize there's a very real chance that the person in front of me might be struggling with loneliness." (Dr. Vivek H. Murthy in Rashid and Brooks, "How to Know You're Lonely.")

14. While the loneliness research can be depressing, the happiness research is equally as encouraging. In the Harvard Study of Adult Development, which is also the longest-running in-depth, longitudinal study of human life ever accomplished, the researchers state that "if we had to take all eighty-four years of the Harvard Study and boil it down to a single principle for living, . . . it would be this: Good relationships keep us healthier and happier. Period." (Robert Waldinger and Marc Schulz, *The Good Life: Lessons from the World's Longest Scientific Study of Happiness* [New York: Simon and Schuster, 2022], 10.)

You are made for people in such a way that you will be lonely if it is just "you and God."

Dwell on that for a moment. It sounds blasphemous: you can be lonely with God.

In Eden, Adam had the one thing you would think he needed, right? You would think that God was sufficient, right? But God himself said, "No, it is not good."

Adam was with the almighty, all-holy, all-fulfilling Trinitarian God of the universe. The one who opens his hand and satisfies the desires of all things.[15] The one who can melt mountains with a word,[16] the one who sings stars into existence.

It is crucial to see that our capacity to be lonely with God is not a sign of God's insufficiency or lack. It is a sign of his unfathomable generosity: God designed us to need people. You cannot experience God the way you were made to until you experience him alongside others.

According to the Almighty himself, God is necessary but not sufficient to the full life of flourishing that he created us for. That is not to say God will not meet us in our loneliness. He will. But as we see with Adam, he will not leave us there either. Because we were made by God for more than God.

Our fullest spirituality is only possible with others. Our intended existence only works in a community. Our highest call is only realized when we pursue it alongside others.

In other words, you need friends to be who God made you to be. Friends are the anatomy of your soul. They are at the core of your longings.

This is why you feel the way you do.

15. Psalm 145:16.
16. Psalm 97:5.

You can be lonely with God.

But why do we act the way we do?

If friendship is built into the DNA of our souls, why do we find it so difficult? Why do we run from it? Why do we hide?

In most Bibles, there is not even a page turn before this glorious vision of friendship in Eden collapses on itself. It happens because of sin, but take note of exactly how:

The world of relationship has only just begun. Adam and Eve have each other, and they have God. They are naked, vulnerable, and feel no shame. They exist in the essence of friendship: to be completely known and completely loved.

What happens next is what we call the fall, and it is the reason everything in the world—including friendship—has a dark side.

Eve is tempted to sin by eating the fruit of the Tree. Not because it looks so delicious. Not because she is rebellious at heart. Not because she is weak or silly or desirous of some human freedom she doesn't have (at least not yet). Don't read our modern notions into Eve's head. Notice, rather, that someone else puts a question into her head: "Did God really say . . . ?"[17] Also notice that she hears this voice when she is alone.

The route of the enemy is always to pull you aside and tell you lies about who you are and who God is. Because you are most vulnerable when you are alone.

---

17. Genesis 3:1. Consider here that the root of all evil in the world is the question in your head that says, *Does God really mean what he says?* That question is a fundamental inversion of worship. We usually call it pride, but it's even bigger than that. It's a doubt or a rejection of God's reality, or sometimes just a sneaking suspicion that we understand the reality that God made better than he does. That somehow, we get it, and God is a little behind our forward thinking. This spark of distrust spoken by the great deceiver is the downfall of both Eve's world and ours.

And it works on Eve. She eats the fruit. So does Adam. And the whole world begins to fall apart. Or, put another way, the whole world begins to crumble and drift into a current of loneliness.

Think about it.

The first thing that happens to Adam and Eve is that they hide from each other—they cover themselves up with fig leaves. And immediately afterward, they hide from God.

THE ROUTE OF THE ENEMY IS ALWAYS TO PULL YOU ASIDE AND TELL YOU LIES ABOUT WHO YOU ARE AND WHO GOD IS. BECAUSE YOU ARE MOST VULNERABLE WHEN YOU ARE ALONE.

This almost seems comic, right? Like a toddler hiding under the bedsheets, positive that his dad doesn't know where he is. It is like that. But you are like that too. So are we all.

This hiding is spiritual before it is physical. It is the sense that we're not quite right, not quite enough, not quite ready to be seen by others and God. Hiding begins as our unwillingness to be seen and then becomes our insistence not to be known—and that is the root of all loneliness.

This current tears the world apart—relationship by relationship.

First, it tears apart our relationship with God. A chapter ago Adam and Eve were naked and unashamed in the fullest sense—they were fully known and fully loved. But in the world of sin, we separate ourselves from God because we are not sure we are lovable, so we don't want to risk being known.

Second, this current tears our relationships with others apart. We see this so clearly in the story of Cain.

Everyone knows this story, and it is easy to judge the first murderer. But I encourage you to pause and consider the relational depth here. Cain is jealous of his brother. Never mind that he's jealous about flocks and fruits. Most of our jealousies would be inexplicable if we tried to put words to them.

What matters is that because of his jealousy, he hides himself from his brother and from God—his face is turned down in the posture of isolation.[18] The current of loneliness has him.

But also notice God's tender pursuit of Cain. When we hide in our jealously and shame—or even murderous rage—God swims out to us! He is *for* us.

Like the loving Father that he is, God pulls Cain aside and speaks a phenomenal word of grace. It's as if God puts a finger under Cain's chin like any good dad would do and says, "Sin is crouching at your door, but thou mayest overcome it."[19] In Hebrew, the phrase "thou mayest" is *timshel*. Timshel is a sign of grace. It is God saying to Cain that an alternate future is possible. He doesn't have to drift in the current. Relationship and reconciliation are possible. Grace means that things don't have to be the way they are now. Walking out of loneliness is an option.

But what does Cain do? He becomes the world's first murderer. Evil wins. The hiding becomes shame becomes isolation becomes violence, and the cycle we know so well is kicked off for the first time in the world. From crimes of passion to mass shootings to the common ways we lash out at the ones we love,

---

18. "So Cain was very angry, and his face was downcast" (Gen. 4:5).
19. Genesis 4:7, my paraphrase, inspired by John Steinbeck's *East of Eden* which can be read as a retelling of the Cain story that focuses on the rich meaning of *timshel* (or "thou mayest") as the possibility to live otherwise.

we are all offspring of Cain now. And we share in the sentence for his crime.

In the wake of the world's first murder, God seeks Cain out again. (Notice again that while our response to sin is always hiding, God's response to sin is always finding.) God says, "I hear your brother's blood crying out to me from the ground."[20] And like a guilty man in front of a judge, Cain stands before God and receives a sentence for the world's first crime: he is sentenced to be a restless wanderer.[21]

Cain rightly understands this as a death sentence.

"No!" he cries. "I will be a restless wanderer. I will be hidden from your face. And anyone who finds me will kill me."[22] Cain understands that going out alone into the world is both spiritually and physically the end of life.

Isn't that interesting? The consequence of sin for Adam, for Eve, for Cain—indeed for all of us—is isolation. And isolation is death. Spiritually and physically.

And that's how the story ends.

Adam and Eve are sent out of the garden of God. Cain is sent away from his fellow man.

Put together, the stories of Adam and Eve and their son Cain are as short as they are tragic. But they are also incredibly illuminating for our modern predicament.

---

20. Genesis 4:10, my paraphrase. Note the blood crying out from the ground. It's possible to have sympathy for evildoers and fierce anger over the victims and the injustice at the same time. This is a tangent but worth it: If you ever struggle with all the evil and pain and wrongness of the fallen world, cling to these words. God does not ignore innocent blood. Even when he extends forgiveness to evildoers. He hears the blood crying out from the ground. You are not the only one who feels something is terribly broken about the world. The one who can fix it also feels it.
21. "You will be a restless wanderer on the earth" (Gen. 4:12).
22. Genesis 4:14, my paraphrase.

We were made for people, but we are cursed to restless wandering. And a key feature of this curse in both stories is that isolation is both the cause and the consequence of our sin.

Loneliness breeds more loneliness. Which is what makes it such a vicious, swirling current.

The Deadly Current of Loneliness

I am a father of four young boys. Last summer, we took a trip to the beach where I found out that my third son, Coulter, absolutely loves the water. While the other boys played in the sand or bodyboarded nonstop, Coulter (who was four at the time) just strapped into his life jacket, ran out into the waves, leaned back, and let the time pass.

This was wonderful, at first, but I quickly realized that every time I looked up Coulter had drifted waaaaay down the shore. Luckily, my wife, Lauren, had bought him a neon-green swim shirt. So I'd jump up, scan the beach for a bright green dot bobbing peacefully in the water, and run what felt like half a mile down the coast to haul him back. Then we'd rinse and repeat. (I promise I'm a good parent.)

Now, this kept happening because—I know I'm about to blow your mind—currents exist.

Currents are the things that inevitably pull us down the shoreline unless we swim against them. And cultures have currents too. Like the most dangerous currents in oceans, cultural currents derive their power from being invisible. Usually, we have no idea we're in a current until it's too late.

We are all much more like Coulter than we think.

Modern culture moves us with a remarkable and silent speed

down the shore of life toward isolation. The easiest thing to do is to do nothing, and like a kid in a life jacket, you will be swept away from the ones you love. Every. Single. Time. Loneliness is where we arrive when we do nothing else. John Stott once wrote that "holiness is not a condition into which we drift."[23] I would add, neither is friendship. Because that's not where the current goes.

How do we drift toward loneliness? The ways are as infinite as they are invisible. We tend to move for jobs, not people. We tend to build back decks, garages, and other architecture that draws us away from one another instead of front porches and sidewalks that push us together.[24] We tend to mediate our relationships with technology (and that may be the wildest understatement of this book).[25] The clubs and associations that formerly gave people myriad intangible connections have now almost entirely disappeared.[26] We tend to gather in front of glowing screens to relax (alone) rather than in front of glowing fires to relax (together).[27] As you can see from the footnotes, entire books have been written about each of these trends. Most of them you probably already recognize.

But what you might not realize is that when all of these are put together, you live in a fierce current.

Which means that to do nothing is actually to do something

---

23. John R. W. Stott, *The Message of Ephesians*, The Bible Speaks Today (Downers Grove, IL: InterVarsity, 1986), 193.
24. Eric Jacobson, *Sidewalks in the Kingdom: New Urbanism and the Christian Faith* (Grand Rapids: Brazos Press, 2003).
25. Andy Crouch, *The Life We're Looking For: Reclaiming Relationship in a Technological World* (New York: Convergent Books, 2022).
26. Robert D. Putnam, *Bowling Alone: The Collapse and Revival of American Community* (New York: Simon and Schuster, 2000).
27. Jennie Allen, *Find Your People: Building Deep Community in a Lonely World* (Colorado Springs: Waterbrook, 2022).

very significant—it is to accept the drift of modern life. The current of modern life is to become busier, wealthier people who used to have friends. And mostly you won't even notice that this is happening. When everyone is drifting in the same current, you won't notice anyone moving at all. If you're going to fight to swim upstream toward a life of friendship, it will look and feel very strange. But loneliness comes without the cost of choice. You don't choose it; it chooses you.

We are not friendless because we want to be. None of us chooses loneliness on purpose. I have never met a single person who does not long wholeheartedly for friendship. But we live with a tremendous dissonance.

It is common sense that friendship is the good life. But common practice is to drift into loneliness.

Why!? Because we live in the world of Cain. We are made for people but cursed to restless wandering. We want friends, but we can't seem to do the one thing we were made for. And like the studies show, it is killing us body and soul.

In the words of Paul, "Who will rescue me from this body of death?"[28]

The death sentence of loneliness is like the enormous waterfall at the end of the current. And as you see in all the cartoons, you never realize you're going anywhere until suddenly you're at the edge of the waterfall and there is nothing you can do.

That is, unless someone who is bigger than you, stronger than you, and who loves you runs down the shore and pulls you out of the water.

That someone is Jesus.

---

28. Romans 7:24 (NET).

Friendship Made Flesh

You may think a lot of things when you hear the name Jesus, but I want you to think of this: Jesus is the ultimate parent who runs down the shore of the world and plucks us out of the current of loneliness.

Baptism has been one of the central sacraments and metaphors for salvation since the beginning of Christianity. Part of the image of baptism is that we are drowning in sin but suddenly raised to new life.[29] This is also a beautiful way to understand the gospel of Jesus: though we were drowning in a world of loneliness, Jesus raised us to a life of friendship.

It may seem odd to cast the story of Jesus' salvation in terms of friendship. But that is exactly how Jesus himself tells it. In his final evening with his disciples, Jesus describes his act of salvation as an act of friendship. "Greater love has no one than this, that someone lay down his life for his friends. . . . No longer do I call you servants, for the servant does not know what his master is doing; but I have called you friends, for all that I have heard from my Father I have made known to you. You did not choose me, but I chose you."[30]

Those words may be familiar. But hear them anew in the context of the story we've been through.

In Eden, we were made for each other, to be fully known and fully loved. But in the fall, this is what we lost. We are not known,

---

29. "Or don't you know that all of us who were baptized into Christ Jesus were baptized into his death? We were therefore buried with him through baptism into death in order that, just as Christ was raised from the dead through the glory of the Father, we too may live a new life" (Rom. 6:3–4). Baptism also connotes the metaphor of being washed clean (Acts 22:16).
30. John 15:13, 15–16 (ESV).

we fear we are not loved, and we run away and hide. Loneliness breeds loneliness, and we are cursed to lives of restless wandering. Much of the Old Testament is the dysfunctional story of what happens when restless wanderers collide. It is the story of a people longing for someone to come and make things right again.

Enter Jesus. Though he was the beloved son of God the Father, he left community and became lonely for us.[31] Though he was without sin, he took on the sentence of a restless wanderer and roamed the world for us.[32] And by doing all this, he reversed the curse of sin and loneliness.

Unlike Eve, when he faced the Serpent's lies, he spoke back with the words of God.[33] Unlike Adam, when tempted to eat and sin, he refused.[34] Unlike Cain, he embraced the *timshel* possibility to do otherwise. He became the older brother we needed,[35] dying alone in our stead, hidden from the gaze of God,[36] all so that we could be raised to a life of community and see the face of God again.[37] In all of this, Jesus took the curse of isolation so that we could become known.

But this good news does not stop at the death of Jesus. In the resurrection, Jesus pronounced the final word of our future—we *will* be raised again to unity with one another and unity with the Trinity. In the meantime, he has sent his Holy Spirit to be "with" us—a lifeline of presence in the current of loneliness.[38]

That Jesus frames the story of salvation in terms of friendship

---

31. Philippians 2:5–8.
32. Matthew 8:20.
33. Matthew 4:10.
34. Matthew 4:4.
35. Mark 3:34–35; Romans 8:29; Hebrews 2:11.
36. Matthew 27:46.
37. 1 Corinthians 13:12.
38. John 14:16.

is one of the most astounding and comforting claims in the Bible. Remember the Trinitarian bash that we began with? Jesus is inviting us into that circle of friends, to celebrate for time eternal. Spiritually speaking, friendship is our final destination.

In light of this story, it makes so much sense why Jesus would describe his act of salvation the way he does: "I have called you friends." The gospel of our salvation in Jesus is not just reflective of friendship—it *is* friendship.

The friendship of Jesus means that one way to summarize the gospel is this: Jesus knows you fully and loves you anyway.

Jesus sees through all the hiding. He sees through the fig leaves of your emotional armor and knows your vulnerabilities. He knows all the reasons you think you are a failure, you think you are inadequate, you think you are full of shame—and he looks at you and says, "I'm sticking with you anyway."

What is a friend if not that kind of person!? A true friend, after all, is someone who knows you that well and decides to stick around anyway.

A friend knows your bad jokes and likes you anyway. A friend knows what you look like when you're grumpy and tired and stays by your side anyway. A friend knows your trauma, your shame, your worst secrets and says the words you desperately need to hear: "I know you. I understand you. And I love you anyway."[39]

Here then is my working definition of friendship for this book: "A friend is someone who knows you fully and loves you anyway."

And that is exactly who Jesus is. Jesus is friendship made flesh.

---

39. I am indebted to Timothy Keller for these observations. They reflect his comments in a sermon given in Richmond in the early 2000s, the recording for which is no longer available online.

Rediscovering Covenant Friendship

It is fascinating that the word *friendship* has gone out of fashion.

"We don't have a word for the opposite of loneliness, but if we did, I could say that's what I want in life."[40] So begins a now famous essay by Marina Keegan. In it, she poignantly describes how we all long for relationship, and yet she gropes for what the word is. This is not new.

> A FRIEND IS SOMEONE WHO KNOWS YOU FULLY AND LOVES YOU ANYWAY.

C. S. Lewis named this problem half a century ago at the beginning of his famous essay on friendship.

> To the Ancients, Friendship seemed the happiest and most fully human of all loves; the crown of life and the school of virtue. The modern world, in comparison, ignores it. We admit of course that besides a wife and family a man needs a few "friends." But the very tone of the admission, and the sort of acquaintanceships which those who make it would describe as "friendships," show clearly that what they are talking about has very little to do with that *Philia* [the Greek word for friendship] which Aristotle classified among the virtues or that *Amicitia* [the Latin word for friendship] on which Cicero wrote a book. It is something quite marginal; not a main course in life's banquet; a diversion; something that fills up the chinks of one's time.[41]

---

40. Marina Keegan, "The Opposite of Loneliness," in *The Opposite of Loneliness: Essays and Stories* (New York: Scribner, 2014), 1.
41. C. S. Lewis, "Friendship," in *The Four Loves*, 73–74.

The word *friendship* has indeed suffered a loss of value. David Benner puts it well: "The coin of friendship has been continuously devalued by being applied to these lesser forms of relationship."[42] This is particularly true in an age of Facebook, which will always have the dubious honor of "turning 'friend' into a verb."[43]

I believe it is the call of the church to reclaim the word *friendship* in all its spiritual depth.

When we understand Jesus' life as an act of friendship, the word suddenly leaps from some luxury on the periphery of life to a necessity at the center of life.

Friendship is not just the word for the opposite of loneliness; it is the word made flesh in Jesus. This means that to become more like Jesus necessarily means to become more and more like a friend. You cannot have a real life of faith without friendship.

So one of my greatest hopes in this book is to give you back this word in all its spiritual power: *friendship*. To do so, I suggest the phrase *covenant friendship* as a way to re-enliven the word *friendship* with the tones of Jesus' life of covenant friendship on our behalf.

The Arts of Covenant Friendship

Jesus is the master of covenant friendship, and this book is about learning the arts of the master, so the chapters will follow the arts as Jesus embodies them.

We will unpack the meaning of covenant friendship in depth in chapter 3, but think of covenant friendship as a way to

---

42. David Benner, *Sacred Companions: The Gift of Spiritual Friendship Direction* (Downers Grove, IL: InterVarsity Press, 2002), 61–62.
43. Alexander Nehamas, *On Friendship* (New York: Basic Books, 2016), 4.

1. VULNERABILITY

2. HONESTY

5. INVITATION

8. COMMUNICATION

9. MEMORY

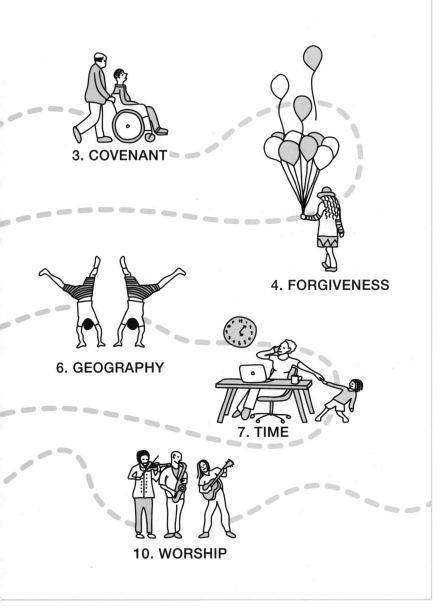

3. COVENANT

4. FORGIVENESS

6. GEOGRAPHY

7. TIME

10. WORSHIP

explicitly name the idea that we were made to be fully known and fully loved over the long haul.

The first part of this definition is the idea of being fully known. We see this in Jesus' words on friendship in John 15. Jesus claims that unlike in a master-servant relationship, he has made everything known to his disciples. He has fully disclosed himself in words. Thus our first two arts of friendship: vulnerability and honesty.

The second part of this definition is that Jesus remains committed. He fully loves over the long haul. In the passage in John, Jesus goes on to say that he "chose" us.[44] He describes this love as someone who is willing to lay down their life for a friend. In this loving commitment, Jesus has forgiven our past and committed to our future. Thus the third and fourth arts of friendship: covenant and forgiveness.

By acting out this covenant friendship to us, Jesus has invited us into the Trinitarian friendship of the Father, Son, and Spirit. Thus the fifth art of friendship, invitation.

From there the embodied arts of covenant friendship get more and more practical. If we are to model covenant friendship as the limited beings that we are, we must consider space and schedules and talking—thus the next three arts of friendship: geography, time, and communication.

We close with two final arts of friendship: memory and worship. Both, we'll see, are ways we invite eternal significance into our friendships the way Jesus did with his friends.

While I think *covenant friendship* is a useful phrase to describe the fully knowing and fully loving relationship Jesus modeled for

44. John 15:16.

us, I don't want to clutter the writing. So throughout this book, I will often just use the word *friendship* with only occasional references to "covenant friendship" for emphasis.

But as you read these pages, let the term *covenant friendship* ring as an echo in the background. The hope of this book is that the life of Christ and the word *friendship* will become so deeply intertwined that the word seems to belong in a category with *quiet time, grace, salvation*, and *prayer*: words that reflect the natural result of a Christian life.

Because that is exactly what friendship is—the relational response to the life of Christ.

Friendship Is Contagious

When I think back to that kid in the hallway some two decades ago, I see myself as someone who longed for the opposite of loneliness and couldn't name it. But I also see the providential hand of Jesus grabbing my arm and pulling me out of the deadly current by binding me to a friend named Steve.

We had no idea how much friendship would change our lives. But it changed everything.

At first, it was a remarkable comfort. So much of the anxiety I thought was baked into life was really baked into loneliness. When someone knows you fully and sticks around anyway, you walk into the world with a strange courage—even when you're playing the clarinet and tucking in your shirt. But by God's grace, this friendship became much more than the companionship of skateboarding and high school mischief.

It became the place we told everything and felt fully known. It became the place we spoke words of honest encouragement and felt fully loved. It was the place where we suddenly became people without secrets, and in that the theory of the gospel of Jesus was made into the real practice of life.

But it also became the place of real problems. Like all friendships, ours has been a place where we have fought, where we have failed, where we have forgiven, and—again by God's grace—where we have forged ahead.

Slowly, what began as a covenant friendship between two people became covenant friendships between many people. Over those years, I have come to believe that covenant friendship is like a fire: in the best of ways, it consumes all of you, and it spreads to others.

Two decades later, Steve and I remain the closest of friends here in Richmond, Virginia. Before that, we both moved away and lived in many places, from Africa to China to Washington, DC, and more. But we both moved back to Richmond, we've both gotten married, and we both have big families. Our wives are friends, our children are friends, and we both have tons of other people we call covenant friends.

Quite a few of those friends live here in Richmond with us. Many don't. But all of us would say that covenant friendship has transformed the way we understand who God is and the way we walk with him.

I want to tell you the stories of how friendship has changed us, but before I do, permit me a note on how to read these stories.

How to Read This Book

In this book, you will read stories about the people whom I call covenant friends. These people are all wonderful, and they are all flawed. They are also normal people who (for the most part) don't care to be written about in a book. So, except where I have explicit permission otherwise, my stories will stay anonymous.

But reading other people's stories can be finicky. So let me say three things very clearly here at the outset.

1. My Stories Are Windows, Not Pictures

First, my stories are not your stories. And they shouldn't be. They are the only way I know how to tell of the grace God has worked in my life through friendship. But they are nowhere close to the whole picture of what God offers us in the gift of friendships. So, at best, I offer them not as pictures you should look at but rather as windows you should look through.

Hearing about my friends in China or our group of friends in Richmond may not make sense of your friends spread out across Central Texas or Northern California. It may not make sense of your struggle to meet people in New York City. Hearing about us in our stage of parenting and busy jobs may not resonate with your empty-nest community or with your college roommates—wherever you are.

Nonetheless, I believe we can learn from one another. And I offer my stories as a witness to what God has done in my life, not as a prescription of what he must do in your life. They are for inspiration, not necessarily imitation.

2. I Write from the Current

Second, I cannot write as an old man with decades of experience. Neither can I write as a theologian or scholar who has studied all of what the Bible and philosophy have to say about friendship. Instead, I write as someone who is trying to swim against the current beside you. I write also as a flawed man who has felt the extraordinary pull of the current of loneliness. And yet I write as someone who has looked up in his late thirties and found friends who are holding me fast. That is a remarkable grace.

I write not in praise of what I have made of my friends but rather in awe of the miracles I have found in them.

3. I Focus on Arts and Habits of Friendship

Finally, as you might suspect, neither miracles nor relationships can be prescribed. Like many important things in life, a lifestyle of friendship is something you have to feel and intuit your way through. Any five-step path to a life of friendship is a terrible lie.

That is why this book will unfold as the arts and habits of friendship.

I use the term *arts* because we should see friendship as something that can never be mastered. Arts are not bullet points you can check off, they are beautiful calls to live into.

And yet to live into any art, we must practice it. So each art is paired with a habit (or two) that we can actually try. Habits are small but significant things you can practice. Little steps that can aggregate into a life of friendship. Friendship never happens in a moment; it is the product of rhythms over time. I include these habits of friendship as a way to honor that reality.

Taken together, think of this arts-and-habits framework as a way to say that while a life of friendship is hard, by God's grace, it is possible. None of these arts or habits are easy. In fact, all of them are hard. Really the only thing that is easy is to ride the current to loneliness. If you are looking for easy, then you'll be swept downstream. But you do not have to live like that.

Jesus has made a way for us, and by learning from his arts and imitating his habits, we can swim upstream.

May the Kingdom of Friendship Come

The other week, Lauren and I spent an ordinary evening talking with some friends. We began at a restaurant and ended next to a fire in our living room. We talked late, caught up on the past, and dreamed about the future. It was not anything extraordinary, or at least it didn't seem like it at the time.

But before I shut off the light and walked to bed, I looked around the living room where we had sat, and I experienced the overwhelming feeling of holy significance. Like I was looking at a cathedral still echoing with the sounds of worship. As if something much more than conversation had just happened.

Friendship makes ordinary life seem sacred.

There is a reason for that. When we practice it, we are in a real sense living into the temple, because together we are the communal dwelling place of God.[45] It's no wonder we feel the presence of God in friendship.

But we are also rehearsing the future God has destined us for.

Many Bibles title chapter 22 of Revelation "Eden Restored," and for good reason. Revelation shows us a description of the coming kingdom in which the garden has become a city. There is a tree of life again, and the curse of Cain is reversed and replaced with a mark of honor on our foreheads—the name of

---

45. "And in him you too are being built together to become a dwelling in which God lives by his Spirit" (Eph. 2:22).

God.[46] In this culmination of human history, we will "see his face"[47] and we will "be his people."[48]

Notice that all of this is plural. Revelation is a party of covenant friends who have become family. Many things about the world will pass away, but the pursuit of friendship is glorious, in part, because it has an eternal quality.

You may be in a place of loneliness now, but that is not your final destination. Jesus will not leave you there. He promises a different future.

So let us do something about it. The practice of friendship is the way we act out the prayer "May your kingdom come."

You were made for friendship. It is what you long for. It's what the whole world needs.

This book is about how to fight for it.

---

46. "Then the angel showed me the river of the water of life, as clear as crystal, flowing from the throne of God and of the Lamb down the middle of the great street of the city. On each side of the river stood the tree of life, bearing twelve crops of fruit, yielding its fruit every month. And the leaves of the tree are for the healing of the nations. No longer will there be any curse. The throne of God and of the Lamb will be in the city, and his servants will serve him. They will see his face, and his name will be on their foreheads" (Rev. 22:1–4).
47. Revelation 22:4.
48. Revelation 21:3.

CHAPTER 1

Vulnerability

The Art of Living without Secrets
and the Habit of Confession

In April during my first year of college at the University of Virginia, I woke one beautiful spring day to a terrible hangover and a phone call. I say day because it was not morning. It was two o'clock on a Saturday. And I can't remember which I noticed first, the pain of my headache or the loud ringing of the phone.

I made it over to the desk on my side of the dorm to answer it, and to my surprise, it was my mother.

She said she was passing through Charlottesville with my little brother and wondered if she might stop by and say hi. Before I even knew what day or time it was, I said of course. Because what else do you say to your mom?

It was when I hung up that I noticed the pain everywhere else. My throat was coarse from smoking too much and my head hurt from alcohol. But there was a discomfort I couldn't put my finger on that made this hangover different.

I ran my hand down my arm, and suddenly an arrow of pain went through my wrist. My memory followed my fingers to the night before.

I saw myself standing in a circle of drunk boys. (I say boys because I tell my sons that you become a man not because of your age or size but rather when you start acting like one.) I remember we passed around Parliaments, taking drags and then stubbing them out on one another's bodies. I looked down at my forearms and saw a burn hole in each of them.

So I got up, threw on a long-sleeved shirt to hide my arms, and walked outside.

I recall it was one of those first truly warm and beautiful days of spring when I stood outside greeting my mom and my little brother, Frank. It was too warm for long sleeves.

I don't remember a single other thing about that meeting except the shame. The shame of having something to hide.

The feeling of hiding moved up my forearms and enveloped all of me.

Sin Wants Us Alone

How did I get to that morning?

By the end of high school, I had a life full of friendships with Steve and the others we would go on to call covenant friends. But as we often must do, I had to leave those relationships to go to college.

This is the nature of life. Sometimes we start over. Often when we do, we find ourselves alone again. These are some of the most dangerous turning points in life. It did not take long for me to deteriorate.

This was not because of any spectacular temptation. For me, college brought all the usual temptations, at least of the flesh. By some grace, ideologically I felt rather well prepared for college. When philosophy professors told me we were nothing but slabs of meat, but that we should act morally anyway, I found them nonsensical. I sincerely felt the Bible I had grown up with had better answers. When Harvard-educated scholars of that Bible told me that you really needed to throw half of it out "historically speaking," I found their arguments uncompelling.

I "believed" in Jesus as much as I ever did. I just didn't want to follow him.

So rather than being tempted into false teachings, I was tempted by the flesh. I felt intellectual forays into faith were best while drunk. I felt conversations were better while smoking. And, of course, above all I was interested in girls.

In some sense, I was an eighteen-year-old college male being tempted by all the usual things. That was not, in itself, significant. What was significant was that I faced all these temptations *alone*. I had no real friends at college (yet) to walk with.

When temptation meets aloneness, temptation wins almost every time.

It is amazing who you can become once you drift away from community. It's also amazing who you can "un-become."

"He who is alone with his sin, is utterly alone."[1] That's the first sentence of Bonhoeffer's chapter on confession in community. And I agree because I've lived it. It's what John Donne called "a torture that hell itself does not threaten."[2]

DO YOU WANT TO KNOW THE LONELIEST WAY TO LIVE? LIVING WITH SIN AND HIDING IT.

Standing on the lawn that morning with my mom, trying to hide my forearms along with everything else about who I had become, I realized something: shame and hiding were becoming the defining features of my life.

1. Dietrich Bonhoeffer, *Life Together: The Classic Exploration of Christian Community*, trans. John W. Doberstein (New York: HarperSanFrancisco, 1978), 110.
2. Philip Yancey, *A Companion in Crisis: A Modern Paraphrase of John Donne's Devotions* (Littleton, CO: Illumify Media Global, 2021), 39.

Do you want to know the loneliest way to live? Living with sin and hiding it.

The Pain of Grace

Remember how gracious God was to Cain? Even in Cain's self-isolating sin, God said, "You may wander, but I'm going to be after you." The hound of heaven has a way of finding us. Very often, that is through a friend. That's what happened to me. God came to find me in the form of a friend. His name was Ken.

I knew Ken from a Christian fellowship that I would come to and sit in the back of, but I didn't know him well. Ken lived in a house with eight other Christian guys. A hilariously messy house of guys who were much more focused on pulling pranks and telling good stories than they were on doing the dishes. It was jokingly named the House of Pain, and guys often said it "hurt so good" to live there. But in more serious moments, the name reflected the truth of real community, that in the pain of exposing our weakness and vulnerability, paradoxically, we become stronger. And true to the name, the vulnerable brotherhood that was happening there was as rich as the carpets were dirty.

Weeks after my moment of shame, Ken approached me and said they needed another person to fill the house next year. I remember telling him I didn't think they wanted someone like me in it. He replied they were all sinners there. I remember thinking about that for a long moment. And then I did something that changed the course of my years in college, something that maybe changed the course of my whole life—I shared what was going on.

That was painful. But it was the intervention of grace I needed to come out of the loneliness of sin and into a community of vulnerability. Ken patiently heard me out and then said I should come live with them anyway.

Pause for a moment and contemplate the grace of Jesus embodied in Ken.

Like the love of God, friendship is not withheld from you because of your mistakes. Don't get me wrong, your mistakes do kill community. They hurt people. They isolate you. They drive you into the desert and make a restless wanderer out of an image bearer. So of course we want to hide these parts of our lives.

But everything changes when we realize that our instinct to hide is not only wrong but also incredibly dangerous. We mistakenly think that hiding keeps us safe by shielding us from danger. But what hiding actually shields us from is love. It may be counterintuitive at first, but consider that we are not happiest when we are hiding and "safe." We are happiest when we are exposed and loved anyway. We are the most human when we are most intimately known. And that means coming out of our hiding places.

This means we need to reframe our view of sin because the enemy has lied to us about our sins. The great deceiver has whispered in our ears, telling us that our sins prevent us from relationship, so we should be ashamed and hide them. Do not believe it.

The truth of grace is that our sins—even our nastiest ones—are not the things that prevent us from being loved. Those very flaws are what make us human, create our need for others, and make our reception of grace possible. And in confessing them we become closer to one another and God than ever before. Honesty about our sins becomes the path, not the barrier, to relationship.

Grace means that your hidden failures are not the end of your story. They can be the beginning of friendship.

The heart of the gospel of Jesus, after all, is that Jesus sees us clearly and loves us dearly. The very core of our salvation is to be exposed and embraced at the same time. This is our spiritual DNA—hiding does not have the possibility to make us happy. On the contrary, being known and loved anyway is the path to happiness, salvation, real life, and real friendship.

> GRACE MEANS THAT YOUR HIDDEN FAILURES ARE NOT THE END OF YOUR STORY. THEY CAN BE THE BEGINNING OF FRIENDSHIP.

Ken embodied this grace of friendship when he invited me into community despite my mess. He showed me that friendship is the place you process your sin in real time. Not the place you go once you're over it.

I will never forget the way the House of Pain invited me in precisely when I was a failure—not after I got better. Yes, it hurt. But doesn't most healing begin that way?

As it turns out, that community would completely reshape my life. Because it was the end of living with secrets. When I tell my testimony, I always point to that year. That was the time when I stopped just "knowing about" Jesus and started following him. Unsurprisingly, following him coincided with being known and being drawn into community.

Vulnerability was the doorway to new life because vulnerability is the doorway to true friendship.

Someone Who Knows Everything

A few years ago, I remember sitting in my living room talking with a close friend when we got a call with some bad news.

Someone we both knew well had become badly addicted to prescription drugs.

What scared us about this story was not the crisis itself. What scared us was that it was happening to someone like us. Someone we expected to be immune to these kinds of crises.

I hear this saying often: "People fall in private long before they fall in public." It always troubles me. The seemingly never-ending line of people whose lives implode from the inside out never ceases to scare me, not only because it is sad but also because it brings things so close to home. *If they hid something like this, who else is hiding? Could I? Would I?*

We are all prone to hide. Part of what it means to be human on this side of the fall is to be comfortable with hiding and pretty good at it. We all seem to have this innate ability to live behind the fig leaves, to pretend everything is going well while things rot from the inside out.

As my friend and I sat shocked and saddened in my living room, I remember we did not ask the usual question: "But how could this happen!?" At some point in my life, I started to expect this stuff more than be surprised by it. Instead, the question we asked each other was, "Is there anything you aren't telling me?"

It was a fascinating moment. We both wondered what would be said next.

Then we both said, "No. You know everything."

This was also a fascinating moment. The pain of knowing that our friend was hurting didn't go away, but I remember feeling free to be sad for him and to pray for him without the self-consciousness of wondering, *Could this happen to me?* Because I had once again attached myself to the lifeline of vulnerability with a friend.

You can be friends with someone for a long time and never really allow them to push you into a corner of honesty with such a question: "Is there anything I need to know?" Or, "Is there anything important you're withholding from me?"[3]

I realize these are very uncomfortable questions. But in the context of love, they are the place where we meet grace.

Think about Nathanael or the woman at the well. Both of these stories in John are places where Jesus reveals to people that he knows them thoroughly but loves them anyway, and both people come away worshiping him.[4] The word *vulnerable* means to be capable of being wounded. This is terrifying—unless surrounded by love. To be fully known without being fully loved is to be exposed. (And to be loved without being fully known is really to be hidden.) But to be fully known and still be fully loved, that is the beginning of worship. Which is why no matter how scary it seems, you need friends who know you completely. Because only then can they start loving you anyway.

No One Is Surprised That You Are a Sinner

Consider this claim: to live as a Christian necessarily means to live into community. That may sound radical, but a Christian who is fundamentally alone is not living as a Christian.

Being made for people means that you're made to be friends with sinners. That goes for you too—people have to be friends

---

3. A fuller version of this story is told in an exploration of the habit of vulnerability in my first book *The Common Rule: Habits of Purpose for an Age of Distraction* (Downers Grove, IL: InterVarsity Press, 2019), 95–103.
4. John 1:43–51; 4:1–42.

with the sinner version of you because that's the real version of you.

This means that vulnerable community is the only real version of Christian community. You cannot have real community without real vulnerability.

This gets to the essence of what it means to live as a body of believers: living with one another in a way that mirrors how we live with Christ. Living as a body of believers is not hiding but confessing. It is not remaining unknown but being fully known so we have the opportunity to be fully loved.

Why, then, is it so hard to confess and be honest and vulnerable!?

The core feature of Christianity is that we are all, wait for it, *sinners!* Why pretend anything else? Hear it from Bonhoeffer: "The pious fellowship permits no one to be a sinner. So everybody must conceal his sin from himself and from the fellowship. We dare not be sinners. Many Christians are unthinkably horrified when a real sinner is suddenly discovered among the righteous. So we remain alone with our sin, living in lies and hypocrisy. The fact is that we are sinners!"[5]

So then, let's talk like we're sinners.

The grace of Jesus is nothing to rejoice about if we cannot first be honest about why we need that grace!

Last night a few friends and I sat on my front porch. There was a heavy rainstorm outside, and we sat watching it while sharing our difficulties in our work lives and marriages—or in one friend's case, in his dating life.

One commonality that ran through the conversation was

---

5. Bonhoeffer, *Life Together*, 110.

our feeling like we were not enough. Not enough to make our wives happy. Not enough to finish all the work of the family. Not enough to figure out the next step in our careers. Not enough to get the sleep we need or the time off we feel like we should take.

As you might expect, we did not solve any of these problems!

We just spent time trading inadequacies, confessing—in the most informal but authentic way—that life is mostly hard.

Yet we did solve something very important. Through the grace of God we warded off, for one more day, the poisonous lie that ruins life, the lie that says, "You are fine on your own—you don't need others. You're better than them anyway."

The glorious irony of friendship is that the vulnerable conversation that doesn't "solve any problems" often solves the real problem. And that, note, was only an hour out of a week. We need much more time sleeping and eating and working, but it's fascinating that just an hour or so of being vulnerable raises us to new life again.

That hour of conversation was simply about being known together, sitting in the "not enough-ness" together, feeling like we had companions on the journey of life's mundane difficulties. It was about experiencing the presence of those who are also inadequate and therefore feeling adequate to carry on.

"If we live for others, we will gradually discover that no one expects us to be 'as gods.' We will see that we are human, like everyone else, that we all have weaknesses and deficiencies, and that these limitations of ours play a most important part in all our lives. It is because of them that we need others and others need us."[6]

---

6. Thomas Merton, *No Man Is an Island* (New York: Harcourt, 2002), xxi.

This is the gospel inversion of attracting people into your life. We become great in other people's lives precisely when we show them how weak we really are. Jesus defeated evil first by dying. He closed the gap between us by suffering. It's the path Jesus went down that allows us to follow him up.

You will see this path in every real friendship. To move up, you first have to move down. Because the way down *is* the way up.

Probably, if you are like the rest of us, all your life you thought that to attract people you had to be strong, be better, be more beautiful, be more everything.

But as it turns out, we want to encounter each other's deficiencies. These are the chinks that make us real people.

Confession, in this sense of sharing deficiencies, is an act of solidarity. The more specific the better. And that is worth dwelling on. The act of being specific in your confessions—which we will call vulnerability—is the act of strengthening friendship.

Here there is a difference between "sharing" and "vulnerability."

The Difference between Sharing and Vulnerability

Friendship requires speaking the language of vulnerability. And that is not necessarily easy. We have been taught a different language all of our lives. I call this the distinction between "sharing" and "vulnerability."

Sharing is what we do to update people on our lives. But vulnerability is what we do to let people into our lives.

There is nothing wrong with sharing. After we share, people know about what is happening in our lives. Sharing is great and useful to a limited extent. But it is like writing your own Wikipedia page—anyone can read it, but that does not mean they know you.

Knowing comes from vulnerability. Sharing is about what happens to us. Vulnerability is about what happens in us. Sharing takes time. Vulnerability takes courage. It may be true that vulnerability cannot happen without sharing, but sharing can certainly happen without vulnerability.

To be vulnerable is to use your words to let someone into the mess of your life.

I was an English major, and one of the first things they teach you about writing is "Show. Don't tell."

For example: "Mary remembered that Jack was a good brother to her," is a boring sentence. It tells us something, but it shows us nothing.

Here's a different example: "Mary never forgot the way her brother Jack would always give her the first piece of his apple, and if she was too scared to sleep, he would lie at the foot of her bed, sometimes all night if she needed him to." Now that is a story! Why?

Because in showing, not just telling, a character suddenly came alive. When we see human beings we can relate to, we are automatically drawn in. And the hallmark of being human is this: flaws.

We are drawn to flaws because *we* have them. This is why talking about our sins instead of hiding them under the sheets is the way to friendship.

The table on the next page gives some examples.

You'll notice that in these "sharing" examples, people are

SHARING	VULNERABILITY
I'm struggling in my marriage.	Our shouting woke up the kids last night, and someone threw something.
I'm really stressed out at work.	I'm taking pills to fall asleep because otherwise, I can't settle down.
I'm struggling with passion in my walk with God.	Ever since I read that book, I'm starting to think that this whole faith is maybe a fiction.
My wife and I are going through a rough patch.	I'm flirting with a colleague on a text chain.

trying to be honest. But by hiding the details, they are hiding themselves. When you talk about your real life, a real person emerges. That is what we're trying to do in vulnerability: be real people to one another. You cannot love an abstract person, but you can love a real one.

I am not saying you should have this level of vulnerability with all people all of the time, of course. People who tell everything all the time to anyone who will listen push other people away rather than bring them closer. People need context, space, and the right environment to hear the whole truth. The truth is a scary and sacred thing. Share it wisely. Boundaries should exist.

I am also not suggesting that anytime is the right time to

be vulnerable. But I am suggesting that vulnerability should come at some regular time to some regular people. Creating and deepening friendships requires this kind of vulnerability and, as we will talk more about in chapter 7 on scheduling, requires it regularly.

So of course you are not telling everyone everything, but you must be telling someone everything. Because vulnerability is the catalyst of friendship.

On Coming out of Hiding

Remember the evening in the living room with my friend?

Well, the very next evening, I heard a knock at the door after everyone had gone to bed. And no, I am not a strange old remnant from another time; I am also a normal person like you who texts before going over and knocking on someone's door. So it was very strange to open the door and see my friend from the night before back on my porch.

He had a terrible look on his face, and the first words out of his mouth were, "We need to talk."

This, too, is a hallmark of vulnerable friendship—it interrupts. Of course I had work, of course I had the kids, of course I had Lauren inside wondering what was going on. But when a friend needs to talk, you pour a drink and sit on the porch and do it.

So that's what we did. And I will never forget what he eventually said: "You remember the question we asked last night about anything we haven't told each other?"

I did. And when he said that, I knew where this was going.

It is one thing to tell the truth at the beginning. It is another thing to tell the truth after you have been hiding or lying or faking it. It takes courage, and it is probably one of the most embarrassing and difficult things imaginable.

I know because I've done it.

So I sat still and listened as this friend did one of the bravest, noblest, and most friend-creating acts that I've ever seen. He told the whole truth.

What he shared was very difficult to hear at first because I had to deal with the pain of being hidden from. Really, of being lied to. That is hard. Anyone who has been in a relationship where they are doing the difficult work of being honest, only to find the other person has been doing the easy work of hiding or lying, feels cheated. Betrayed. Alone. Scared, and worse. You can doubt the whole universe. *Has everyone I've ever known been lying to me? Is anyone really honest? Am I the only one who wants to be?*

This is normal. But speaking from experience, I encourage you to let those thoughts fade and instead enter into the joy of what has now happened: someone was honest. Someone was vulnerable. And this changes everything.

It did for us.

That night was a turning point in my friend's life, in our relationship, and in my understanding of friendship.

It changed his life because he never would have been able to leave his struggle without confessing it. But he told it. And he left it. That's a miracle.

It is also worth noting that what felt like a terrifying moment of vulnerability for him looked like an incredible act of bravery to me.[7] Of course you are afraid to tell your secrets. But what

---

7. Brené Brown, *Daring Greatly: How the Courage to Be Vulnerable Transforms the Way We Live, Love, Parent and Lead* (London: Portfolio Penguin, 2013). Brown has excellent research-based insights into how "shame derives its power from being unspeakable,"

has anyone ever gained from hiding except shame? Moments of vulnerability are powerful because they take our shame and turn it into courage.

That night changed our relationship because there is a depth friendship cannot go to until you know the real flaws of someone else. And you get there only by telling the truth. Humans telling the truth instead of hiding—that, too, is a miracle. This is the great paradox of friendship: What we hide pushes people away. What we share draws them in.

It changed my life too. I see now that the route to friendship is not around our failures. It is through them.[8] That means we have second chances. Lots of them. You may have been hiding for a long time. You may have even lied about hiding. But it is never too late to come out of your hiding. Your friends and your heavenly Father are waiting to receive you with joy.

The Habit of Confession

Living into the art of vulnerability requires practicing the habit of confession.

This can be done in different ways, but let me share with you one way a friend and I have been doing it recently. Every Monday night, Steve calls me. And we go through a script he

---

but what feels like weakness to us looks like courage to others. And this makes vulnerability contagious.

8. "Vulnerability is the state we must pass through in order to deepen our connection with God and others. . . . There is no other way." (Curt Thompson, *The Soul of Shame: Retelling the Stories We Believe about Ourselves* [Downers Grove, IL: InterVarsity Press, 2015], 123.)

wrote that lives on a note in our phones. It goes something like this:

> **Caller:** How are you?
> **Listener:** I'm good. Thanks for calling. Why do we call?
> **Caller:** Because it is good to tell someone who loves us the things that burden us.
> **Listener:** What has burdened you this week?
> **Caller:** *Confesses the big and small things, in brief but real detail.*
> **Listener:** Thank you for sharing. Have you left anything unsaid?
> **Caller:** *If yes, tells more. If not:* No. You know everything.
> **Listener:** Good. If there is more unsaid, you can say it the next time we speak.
> **Caller:** Thank you for listening. You help carry a burden that is too heavy alone.
> **Listener:** You are welcome. I am with you, and Christ loves you unconditionally.
> *Switch roles. And then both say goodbye.*

As you might imagine, the first few times we did this, it was a bit halting, and we both had to look at our notes. But as I often remind people, nothing is normal until it is. The habits that reshape our lives take practice, and so it is with the habit of confession.

Now, it is a framework we indwell. A usual Monday night

with a quick call. It takes five minutes or less, but that tiny habit means a life without secrets. And that makes all the difference.

A Life without Secrets

A few weeks ago, as I was lying in bed about to fall asleep, my wife, Lauren—totally out of the blue—asked, "You're not keeping any secrets, right?"

What a question! And what a brave woman to ask it on an otherwise normal Tuesday night. At the time I thought it was random, but I later learned that she had talked to a friend whose husband decided to leave her (and their many children) after years and years of marriage. All because of something he was hiding.

I see now why she was lying awake thinking about that pain.

I love that she had the courage to ask it of me. I loved even more that I could roll over, take her hand, and say what I said: "No. I'm not. I work every day—for you and for our boys—to make sure I live without secrets. And I'm keeping it that way."

This is not to say my life is perfect or even pretty. I cannot say I don't have big mistakes, big problems, or serious issues. I have all those things and more. But I can say that I write as a man without secrets. And in that vulnerability with others I experience the tangible love of Jesus.

I couldn't do that without covenant friends.

CHAPTER 2————————————————————————————————

Honesty

The Art of Saying What You Mean and the
Habits of Rebuke and Encouragement

Do you always just say what you mean? I thought as I sat at a stone table in a garden on the campus of a Chinese university. My friend—who will remain anonymous—sat across from me, telling me rather bluntly about how I needed to work on my organizational skills. Our Bibles were beside us, covered in brown paper to hide the fact that they were Bibles. (We were both American missionaries in China, which by nature meant we were "undercover.") I was twenty-two, living on the other side of the world, and terrible at keeping a planner. I knew he was right.

My friend was a fellow missionary, and if he was good at anything, he was good at telling the truth. Depending on the situation, this made him very blunt, often insightful, many times awkward, and sometimes downright hilarious. But times like this, when he was courageous enough to name a flaw you had, were a combination of very painful and strangely loving.

What strikes me now in retrospect is that this man was a good enough friend to tell me the truth I was blind to. It wouldn't have worked so well if he hadn't told me the truth about the good things too. But his encouragements were as blunt as his rebukes.

A decade and a half later, as a corporate lawyer whose job is to both relate to my clients *and* keep up with the details of their problems, I'm so grateful he encouraged me in my skills and challenged me in my weaknesses. I have him to thank for much growth in my life.

Having a friend who loves you enough to tell you the truth is rare. But honesty is the art of a true friend.

If vulnerability means having the courage to speak the truth about yourself, then honesty means having the courage to speak the truth about someone else.

This art of friendship can be broken into two habits—encouragement and rebuke. Both take honest words; one to name the good, the other to name the danger.

The Power of Words in Friendship

Consider that the divine power of God given to Adam in Genesis 2 is the authority to name the world. Naming the animals is not secretarial work. Remember, in the context of Genesis, God has just created the very existence of the world through words. Words brought reality to life.

Thus, God's request for Adam to name the world is not delegation of an administrative task nearly so much as it is passing the baton of a fundamental power—to create realities by speaking words.

The power to name is the power to create reality. Or, on the flip side, to change, tear down, or destroy realities.

The power of words is a double-edged sword. "The tongue has the power of life and death," the Proverbs say.[1] With words we can build incredible things in people, and we can also tear things down. That is not to say there is one good thing (building) and one bad thing (tearing down). In the created order, both are good things, but in the fallen world we inhabit, both can be used for bad.

---

1. Proverbs 18:21.

When we build up a false narrative in someone by telling them something nice when it is not really true, that is not encouragement, but a lie. That's what the Proverbs call the "kisses of an enemy."[2] Consider for example telling a friend who is plainly tone-deaf that he or she has a real talent at singing and should pursue it as a career. This would be using the power of encouragement as a lie and setting the friend up for life's most painful work—a failed dream.

On the other hand, it is easy to see the danger of criticism without love. For example, telling your friend who's wrestling with an addiction that they're a mess and will always be one. Naming a reality without naming any alternate future is not rebuke, but cruelty.

But when practiced rightly, encouragement and rebuke have the twin power to push back the fallenness in our lives and build up the righteousness. If you have ever watched a home renovation, you know that you have to tear down the bad before you can remake the good. This is how the Word made flesh uses words: to renovate our hearts and make us new.

Jesus is the master of words in friendship. Jesus not only embodies the vulnerability of disclosure we talked about in the last chapter ("everything that I learned from my Father I have made known to you") but also uses the honest words of encouragement *and* rebuke to call his friends forward. Recall the powerful words of encouragement Jesus uses when he names his friend and says, "I tell you that you are Peter, and on this rock I will build my church." But recall also the equally stark rebuke with which Jesus confronts Peter when he says, "Get behind

2. Proverbs 27:6 (ESV).

me, Satan!" Both of these powerful words happen in the same conversation because Jesus knows how to use words to renovate a life for the kingdom.[3]

If Jesus is comfortable using the power of honest words to build up the good and tear down the bad in his friends, we should be too.

The art of honest words is a way to reflect the image of God, to be a friend like Jesus, and to renovate lives for the kingdom.

The Renovation of Words

One of the recurring claims of this book is that by doing nothing we do something very significant: we drift into loneliness. We can see this reality in the art of honesty because the far more normal thing to do is simply be silent.

With encouragement, we are often afraid of the intimacy that follows. What we feel after offering genuine encouragement is usually best described as awkwardness. But on a deeper level, I believe what we are unused to, and thus scared of, is love itself. We don't know what to do with nonsexual love, which makes us bad at friendship.

With rebuke, on the other hand, we are often afraid of being judgmental. Our cultural moment thinks of friends as the people who are nonjudgmental when it comes to our flaws. We like to keep them around because they "accept us as we are." But that assumes that "who we are" is the same as "who we should be." It assumes that following our hearts will lead us to good places. The only problem is that those are wildly dangerous

---

3. Matthew 16:18, 23.

assumptions. When the honesty we need is seen as judgment we should avoid, we are in a really bad spot.

The biblical version of who we are is much more honest and much more nuanced. Yes, we are fearfully and wonderfully made (we deserve encouragement),[4] but our hearts are also deceitful above all else (we need rebuke).[5] We are image bearers who are fallen and being made new.[6] We're not a house that needs to be torn down, but we are a house that needs serious, serious renovation. We need the renovation of words—the encouragement and rebuke of friends.

This kind of honesty is a rare art. It is much easier to be silent and change the subject. True encouragement can be downright awkward. True rebuke can be downright painful. But to cultivate these habits is to cultivate the art of friendship itself. Let's look at both.

The Art of Naming the Danger through the Habit of Rebuke

Sitting in the garden that day with my missionary friend, listening to him tell me how bad I was at organization, I wasn't mad so much as surprised. Most of us are unused to someone taking the liberty to describe our flaws, and we're even more unused to them telling us to change those flaws. So I was taken aback. But I was not offended. And this is an important distinction. I was, in a strange way, very interested in what he had to say. Because I could see that he was naming a problem in order to call me

---

4. Psalm 139:14.
5. Jeremiah 17:9.
6. Genesis 3; Romans 6:1–4; Revelation 21:5.

forward into a better version of myself. And that he was doing so out of love. This was countercultural to a lot of my experience in life, but it was normal among my community in China, which was one of the most important things I learned from my time there.

For anyone who has experienced it, having someone name problems in your life can be breathtakingly freeing. That is, if you trust them and you're practiced at hearing it.

By the time I moved to China immediately after graduating from college, I was familiar with the way vulnerability catalyzes friendship (as described in the previous chapter). But one of the things I'm forever grateful that my community in China taught me is the way that honest words are the logical follow-up to vulnerability for those who are interested in becoming more like Jesus.

Earlier we described the grace of Jesus as knowing you fully and loving you anyway, which is what a friend does. But as we often say at our church here in Richmond, the loving grace of Jesus finds you where you are but never leaves you where you are.[7] Here is an apparent paradox of grace: the same love that accepts you as you are can also tell you to change. Because real love is for your good, not for your comfort.

THE LOVING GRACE OF JESUS FINDS YOU WHERE YOU ARE BUT NEVER LEAVES YOU WHERE YOU ARE.

---

7. I tip my hat to my pastor Corey Widmer here who makes sure to repeat this every few sermons. He also made sure to let me know that he is paraphrasing the ever-quotable Anne Lamott, who wrote, "I do not understand the mystery of grace—only that it meets us where we are and does not leave us where it found us."

Friends in China embodied this truth to me. I think of the evenings with my roommate John, drinking Belgian beers at a Shanghai pub and sharing with him the difficult parts of my relationship with Lauren—to whom I had recently become long-distance engaged while she was still in college. I first met John the day my plane landed in China. But after just a month or two of vulnerable friendship, he told me one night that if I didn't learn to do the dishes then I'd be a bad roommate (he used more colorful language, as I recall) for the rest of my life, and even worse, I'd be a bad husband because I didn't know how to serve anyone. I never forgot that! I often think about it now and remind myself that a man serves the people he lives with, in big and small ways, and dishes aren't beneath me.

I remember also my friend Cam, whom I got to know at 3:00 a.m. in a restaurant in Hanoi, Vietnam. We were traveling with a group around Asia for vacation one week, and Cam and I found ourselves staying up half the night, engrossed in telling each other about what our lives were really like, the temptations we faced, and the hopes we had for the future. In the wake of those conversations, too, was a lot of honesty, this time in the form of accountability and calling each other to better choices.

I could go on, but I recall over and over how in that time honest rebuke became the flip side of loving vulnerability. When we embody the way Jesus accepts us unconditionally, then we can be vulnerable; and when we embody the way Jesus calls us forward, then we can also speak the honest words of rebuke.

Rebuke can be serious without being harsh. "How long are you going to keep doing this before it ruins your family?" "You need to stop going to her house." "You need to quit drinking."

YOU CANNOT EXPERIENCE GOD THE WAY YOU WERE MADE TO UNTIL YOU EXPERIENCE HIM ALONGSIDE OTHERS.

These are all sentences I have found myself saying to various friends in recent years. They may seem blunt, but in each case, there was a relationship of vulnerability, a back-and-forth of mutual sharing of sins and confession, and then, at points, the place for honesty and saying what you mean.

This presumes, of course, that you actually know and love each other. Rebuke without committed understanding is not real love but a mockery of it. I think of Proverbs 26:18–19, which says that "like a maniac shooting flaming arrows of death is one who deceives their neighbor and says, 'I was only joking!'"

To rebuke someone lightly, or to name their flaws without being very sure that you won't need to take the words back, is like firing off arrows without care. The wounds of a friend are faithful, but the wounds of a fool are deadly, so we shouldn't take them lightly.[8]

That said, we don't have to be perfect in our rebukes. Grace means we can hear people out even if they're not right. My wife, Lauren, and I have an agreement about driving. We are always allowed to shout "Watch out!" or "Red light!" to the other, even though 99 percent of the time the driver already saw the danger or the red light. We made an agreement to say thank you for things like that because the one time it matters, it could be a matter of life and death.

Once we understand who we really are, and that our true hearts and desires can be one of the most dangerous things about us, that's when, we will look for friends who are like Jesus, who will find us as we are but never leave us as we are, and who will love us enough to speak a word of loving rebuke.

---

8. "Wounds from a friend can be trusted, but an enemy multiplies kisses" (Prov. 27:6).

The Art of Naming the Good through the Habit of Encouragement

If rebuke is being honest enough to call someone's attention to a dangerous reality that should be avoided, encouragement is being honest enough to call someone's attention to a good reality that should be cultivated. This is much more than complimenting. It means naming the good that exists and putting courage in one another to seek it.

A couple of years ago, I was talking with a friend on my front porch whom I liked but did not know all that well. We had mutual friends and increasingly realized we had a lot in common, but it was only our first or second time hanging out and talking just the two of us. After a while, this friend said something to the effect of, "It seems like something is happening here," and I responded with something like, "Maybe we should try to be intentional with this friendship."

Let's pause there. If this feels a bit awkward to you, it's because it is. At least a little. Most significant moments are, but that is, in part, what makes them significant. In this case, neither of us was complimenting the other, we were simply naming a good reality and encouraging each other toward it. In the wake of that conversation, we did indeed begin to meet more frequently and more "on purpose." Years later, we still call each other covenant friends, and our friendship can be traced back to a moment of speaking the good on purpose.

Naming a good reality, calling attention to it, is no ordinary action. We call this encouragement because it has a way of causing you to "take heart" or even "take courage." The same fear of hurting someone's feelings that causes us to be silent and not rebuke can manifest in not naming the good either because we fear awkwardness. But on the other side of silence is the heart and courage we need to pursue meaningful realities.

Sometimes this happens in ways that are less formal and sound more complimentary. When I think of my friends, I can hear regular echoes of compliments and encouragements that are often handed out. Some of my friends are great at giving financial advice, some are great at sharing thoughts on politics, some are good at sparking spiritual reflection, some are good at hosting, some are good at giving workout advice, and some are good at working on cars. One thing that I appreciate about my friends is that these things are spoken. If you were to hang out with us or join a text chain, to be sure, you would get made fun of plenty. (I'm still trying to explain to my wife how gibing is a love language for guys, and she should expect our four boys to do it to one another often.) But you would also hear a seriously countercultural current of conversation, and that is naming the good in one another's lives.

> IF REBUKE IS BEING HONEST ENOUGH TO CALL SOMEONE'S ATTENTION TO A DANGEROUS REALITY THAT SHOULD BE AVOIDED, ENCOURAGEMENT IS BEING HONEST ENOUGH TO CALL SOMEONE'S ATTENTION TO A GOOD REALITY THAT SHOULD BE CULTIVATED.

I think the greatest forms of encouragement, however, usually do not come as mere compliments about present characteristics. I believe the deeper form of encouragement is calling a friend to a future possibility—to name a talent they have but at the same time to exhort them to steward and multiply it. Often these are mixed with words of caution, because our greatest virtues are often our greatest vices too.

For example, my friends have often given me rebukes and encouragements in the same conversation. I can think of one recently: a friend told me that I had a gift of communicating to other people and should steward that, but he also told me to be careful not to take on more responsibility than my life stage had space for. A good was named, a danger was identified, and I was called to one and cautioned against the other. What a gift that moment was, and what a gift we give when we practice this as a habit toward the people in our lives.

Any counselor knows that a childhood can be made or broken based on the words spoken by a parent to a child. We do our children an unreplaceable good when we make a habit of saying things like, "I am proud of you," "You are great at this," "You are beautiful," "You are so funny," "I love it when you . . ." and so on. Our hearts are forever looking for love, and when a parent gives the encouragement of love on a regular basis, they send their children out into the world in strength because now those children don't need to look for love, they can give it.

Often when I pray for my sons at night, I give them a blessing over their bodies, and I pray that "their mouths would speak encouragement."[9] I pray this in no small part because I know the power of encouragement can change someone's life.

9. See this full blessing in my book *Habits of the Household*: "Jesus, bless their feet, may they bring good news. Bless their legs, may they carry on in times of suffering. Bless their backs, may they be strong enough to bear the burdens of others. Bless their arms to hold the lonely, and their hands to do good work. Bless their necks, may they turn their heads toward the poor. Bless their ears to discern truth, their eyes to see beauty, and their mouths to speak encouragement. Bless their minds, may they grow wise. And finally, bless their hearts, may they come to love you—and all that you have made—in the right order. Amen." (*Habits of the Household: Practicing the Story of God in Everyday*

Friends can carry on this work in a serious and meaning-ful way.

You may think your friend is confident enough and doesn't need your encouragement. But it is not true. I get to close deals as a lawyer and speak to audiences as an author, but nowhere do I crave encouragement more than with my friends. Because they are the ones who really know me. And when they say, "Keep writing, you're doing good," or, "Keep being patient, your chil-dren need you," or, "Keep getting into the gym, you know it's good for you," those encouragements and exhortations create a path forward. The words of friends create life.

Honest Conversation as a Foundation of Friendship

What does this look like day to day? It begins, practically, with creating a life of conversation.

Conversation is a foundation of friendship. Seeing conver-sation as a centerpiece of friendship pushes back on the idea that common interests alone are the foundation of friendship. While friendships begin with common interests, the kind of covenant friendships that are the subject of this book will eventually turn from love of the common interest to love of the other. And this is an important distinction. Because no matter how much time you spend with someone, or how many common activities you share, if vulnerability and honesty are not practiced regularly such that you turn from loving your shared hobbies to loving each other, then you are not in a friendship but a companionship.

This is one place where I will risk disagreeing with C. S.

Family Rhythms [Grand Rapids: Zondervan, 2021], 199.)

Habits for Honest Conversation

PRACTICE THE TURN IN CONVERSATION

Many of my great friends have the same habit. After twenty minutes of conversation, they say something like "So, how are you?" This is a bit of a speed bump, but it separates the casual conversation of acquaintances from the deep, honest conversation of friends. You will develop your own words for turning conversations, but practice taking the turn as much as possible.

PURSUE SMALL GATHERINGS

I love large gatherings. Whether it is a feast with friends, a big party, or a church conference, there is an energy that is irreplaceable. That said, ideally, such large gatherings should catalyze smaller ones where honest conversation can happen. Think about this in your church. You want people to be pushed toward intimacy, not anonymity. Services should push people to small groups. Small groups should push people to accountability groups. Even in your friend circles, be sure to look for times where smaller conversations can happen and honesty can be pursued.

LEAVE SPACE IN ACTIVITY TIMES

Many of your friendships may be based on shared activities. Volunteering together, working together, or going to the gym together can be the real basis for beautiful friendships. But do not let shared activity displace the soul-deep need for honest conversation. Plan a coffee after the run. Schedule a happy hour after work. Have a breakfast before you go to volunteer. Or perhaps center your hangout around a long walk. These habits of leaving space for conversation turn good companions into real friends.

PRACTICE ASKING QUESTIONS (AND THEN BE QUIET)

One of the great arts of honest friendships is asking good questions. Often this can be combined with the habit of making the turn in conversation. But I encourage you to practice asking a good question and then being quiet and listening. Too many questions can suffocate, but one good question plus a listening ear creates the soil of conversation where vulnerability and honesty can grow.*

EXAMPLES FOR PROMPTING LOVING REBUKES

Sometimes this kind of conversation can be so foreign to our modern tongues that we don't know where to start. Here are some examples to start:

- "I would caution you to look out for . . ."
- "I have noticed you keep saying . . ."
- "Be careful, friend, because . . ."
- "I think you may be missing . . ."
- "This doesn't sound like you at your best . . ."

EXAMPLES FOR PROMPTING ENCOURAGEMENT

Here are some examples of ways to make encouragement normal in conversation:

- "I am always so impressed that you . . ."
- "I'm inspired by the way you . . ."
- "You are so good at . . ."
- "I see the Lord working in you . . ."
- "You did so well when you . . ."

---

* For fascinating research on asking good questions and how they can lead us into honesty and relationship, see Warren Berger's *The Book of Beautiful Questions* (New York: Bloomsbury Publishing, 2018), 103.

Lewis—admittedly a dangerous business. Lewis distinguishes friends from lovers by saying that the posture of friendship is not face-to-face but facing out to something else. "Lovers are always talking to one another about their love; Friends hardly ever about their Friendship."[10] I disagree. I think there is a real face-to-face nature of people pursuing friendship. This includes talking about the friendship, but that is a conversation we'll have in chapter 3 on covenant. For now, the table on the previous page describes some ways to start practicing.

For the purposes of honesty, it's worth saying that this art cannot be cultivated unless there is a rich habit of face-to-face

---

10. C. S. Lewis, "Friendship," in *The Four Loves* (San Francisco: HarperOne, 2017), 78.

conversation. In everyday practice, this means creating space for the kinds of conversation rhythms that allow us to practice the hard work of vulnerability and honesty.

Ebenezers of Honesty

I got to practice this art recently when I saw my old friend Ken, the one I told you about, during a short trip with my wife to New Orleans. Lauren and I were celebrating our fifteenth anniversary, but we still made time to stop by and see Ken and his wife, Mel, for a few hours at their house in a neighborhood off St. Charles.

It was a beautiful few hours. We had tacos and margaritas and remembered all the times we've shared, catching up on life and dreaming about living in the same city again.

Ken dropped us off back near our hotel, but before he left, because I felt I had to, I took Ken by the shoulders, looked him in the eye, and said, "You must know, you changed my life all those years ago when you were a friend to me."

For me, that was a small act of encouragement, of saying what I meant. A way to acknowledge that we both know our time to be friends on a day in, day out basis has passed, but to still name a reality. To solidify in his memory and mine, as an act of worship to the God who created friendship, that we had something.

Such words can be an Ebenezer. I hope those words were.

As image bearers, we are called to use that creative power of words to build redemptive realities. We can do that by telling the truth to our friends—about the bad *and* the good things in their lives.

CHAPTER 3

Covenant

The Art of Commitment and the

Habit of Making Promises

A few years ago, I had the honor of being a groomsman in my friend Barrett's wedding. It was a marvelous one. A bright but cool day at an old farmhouse on the James River where the back lawn stretched out to the water.

There were countless memorable things about that day, but the part I remember even more than the manhattans on the lawn while the sun set over the James River was Barrett's gift to us groomsmen.

In a small stone cottage, Barrett lined up unopened bottles of Scotch on a stone windowsill and gave a small toast to being friends over the long haul. After all, he was getting married and committing to the long haul. He needed us. He wanted us—not just on that day but on all the ones to follow.

Then he presented each of us with one of the bottles. Now, I like Scotch, but the important part wasn't the Scotch. It was what was written on top of the box.

"Here," Barrett said, "this is for you." I looked at the box—the numbers two, zero, three, and five were written in black marker across the top.

"What's this," I asked, "a code?"

He smiled. "That's 2035. The year we will drink this together. You can't open it until then."

I remember both the honor and the awkwardness of it. On the one hand, it was a gift over time. An audacious claim on the future. My future! We had known each other for barely two years, but here was the bold assertion that almost twenty years from now, we'd still be close enough, friends enough, well enough, and around enough to sit down and enjoy a glass together and do what we do best—just talk.

I loved it. But it was also an awkward assumption. Because, after all, who knows what the future might hold. Would we still be friends? Would we still like each other? Would we be in the same city? There were so many questions.

There are always so many questions. Life is totally uncertain, but friendships do not have to be. That is why gestures of commitment are an art of covenant friendship.

The Spirituality of Promising

G. K. Chesterton once wrote that when we make a promise, we make an appointment with ourselves in the future.[1] There is a holy foolishness to that.

One leveling fact of being human is that none of us know what tomorrow will bring. All of us face the future with a real powerlessness. Whether we admit it or not, we are vulnerable in the face of time.

We try to numb this enormous uncertainty by either controlling or coping. We assume "control" over the future and try to manage our uncertainty by planning for all contingencies. But it's hard to worship God while you're pretending to be him, which is why Jesus condemns this kind of person in Luke 12.[2] In

---

1. "The man who makes a vow makes an appointment with himself at some distant time or place." (G. K. Chesterton, *The Defendant* ([New York: Dodd, Mead and Company, 1902], 20, https://www.google.com/books/edition/The_Defendant /8WpaAAAAMAAJ?hl=en&gbpv=0.)
2. "And he told them this parable: 'The ground of a certain rich man yielded an

the other case, we say, "I don't even want to think about it," flee responsibility altogether, and find our comfort elsewhere. One way to avoid relying on God is to avoid relying on anything at all and just check out. This is the opposite of the advice in Proverbs.[3]

Neither fight nor flight is faith. Faith means we live with a painful acknowledgment that everything about the present is uncertain, and yet we act in light of a good future that we believe is certain.

This, after all, is what God did for us. Consider the reality of our salvation: though we were still sinners, Christ died for us.[4] That is to say that despite the mess of our present circumstances, Jesus took an action to secure a future. That future is not here yet, but the promise of it changes everything about the present! Now, the truest thing about a Christian is not the mess of brokenness we find ourselves in but the beautiful future to which we are destined.

This is the spirituality of promising. When we make and keep promises, we reflect the redemptive power of God's covenant in all sorts of small and beautiful ways. Look at the world

---

abundant harvest. He thought to himself, "What shall I do? I have no place to store my crops." Then he said, "This is what I'll do. I will tear down my barns and build bigger ones, and there I will store my surplus grain. And I'll say to myself, 'You have plenty of grain laid up for many years. Take life easy; eat, drink and be merry.'" But God said to him, "You fool! This very night your life will be demanded from you. Then who will get what you have prepared for yourself?" This is how it will be with whoever stores up things for themselves but is not rich toward God.' Then Jesus said to his disciples: 'Therefore I tell you, do not worry about your life, what you will eat; or about your body, what you will wear. For life is more than food, and the body more than clothes'" (Luke 12:16–23).

3. "To humans belong the plans of the heart, but from the LORD comes the proper answer of the tongue. . . . Commit to the LORD whatever you do, and he will establish your plans" (Prov. 16:1, 3).

4. "But God demonstrates his own love for us in this: While we were still sinners, Christ died for us" (Rom. 5:8).

through this lens and you will see the glory of small promises everywhere:

In the vows of marriage, we say amazing things to each other, naming the unpredictability of our fates—for richer or poorer, in sickness and in health—and we commit to loving anyway.

When a dad leans over a crib and says, "I'll always be here for you," he means it. And that promise is made powerful when, years later, that same dad is exasperated by the adolescent stage and exhausted from the weight of work but nevertheless holds to his promise and sticks around to love.

As a business lawyer who writes contracts for a living, I see the hidden power of promising every single day. Most people don't think about the spirituality of a contract and the way God is redemptively at work in small economic promises, but the fact is the world would not—it could not—carry on if we didn't engage in small and large commitments to one another all the time. In mortgages, in loans, in credit card transactions, in warranties and return policies, we constantly rely on one another's promises that we'll pay and provide in the future. Without this amazing and invisible network of constant promising, the world would grind to a halt and human flourishing along with it.[5]

The world would be a miserable and dangerous place to live without the redemptive power of the promises we make. Without covenant, we are at the mercy of our future selves, living as if we could never count on the kind of person we might become, a fate Chesterton calls a "horrible fairy tale."[6]

---

5. This section shouldn't be taken as glossing over the problems of human economic systems. Yet enormous common grace is present in our day-to-day economy of trust in one another's promises. Even amid our problems, it is something to be thankful for.
6. Chesterton, *Defendant*, 21.

Promising, in a real sense, is an identity anchor. Holding us to the kind of person we ought to be in the future.[7]

This divine capacity to promise can and should be a real part of spiritual friendships.

Promising in Friendship

Promising in friendship is a terribly dangerous business.

Life is an ocean of uncertainty. Friendship over the long haul is the same. We have no idea what pain and suffering will come. We have no idea what pettiness or conflict might consume us. We have no idea who we will be and who this person we call a friend will be in the future.

So we might fairly wonder, *With all this danger, why do it?*

Because covenant takes messy things and makes them beautiful. To promise friendship is to fight for an island of trust and stability in this ocean of uncertainty called life. To be a friend is to stand together facing all this mess of life and say, "Instead of letting the future shape our friendship, let's work to make this friendship shape our future." It is an act of faith. This is why we need more—not less—promising in friendships.

But when we avoid making promises in friendship, we do the opposite. We implicitly say that we'd rather have options

---

7. On January 7 and January 21, 1983, Lewis Smedes published two successive articles in *Christianity Today*. The first is on forgiveness as the way to deal with the past, and the second on promising as the way to deal with the future. They are both marvelous, and their pairing has informed my pairing of the next two chapters. See Lewis B. Smedes, "Forgiveness—The Power to Change the Past," *Christianity Today*, December 1, 2002, www.christianitytoday.com/ct/2002/decemberweb-only/12-16-55.0.html; and Lewis B. Smedes, "Controlling the Unpredictable—The Power of Promising," *Christianity Today*, December 1, 2002, www.christianitytoday.com/ct/2002/decemberweb-only/12-16-56.0 .html.

than commitment. Instead of walking in faith toward biblical freedom (the ability to do what we were made for), we walk in fear toward American freedom (the ability to choose what we want). The problem is that real freedom is not the ability to choose what you want in any given moment. Real freedom is the ability to do what you were made for and choose the good.

When we avoid commitment because we want to be able to choose again tomorrow, we're acting out of faith in ourselves, that we're the kind of people who will choose well tomorrow. The fact is, we usually aren't.

The art of covenant is scary because it puts faith in God's provision over our options, but it is also the art of making beautiful places of relationship in a fallen and difficult world. It begins with learning how to name these places of relationship.

The Art of Naming Covenant Friendships

Steve and I accidentally stumbled upon this providential power when we stood in the hallway and named that we were "best friends."[8] Neither of us had any idea that our conversation car-

---

8. I will say now that I no longer think the term *best friend* is the most useful word to describe the kind of friendships I'm talking about. It has the connotation of ranking people, and some inherent exclusivity comes along with that. It is certainly a high

ried a weight of power great enough to bring us out of isolation and into one of the most formative relationships in our lives.

We became unique friends in no small part because we gave that friendship a name. Naming a friendship, in and of itself, can be a great act of commitment. I have seen this happen in many relationships ever since.

A few years later, that friendship with Steve had grown into a mutual network of about ten or so friends with whom we constantly hung out. In some ways, this was just a lucky stroke of having a group of friends who were all in youth group and high school together. We were miscreants getting into all kinds of trouble. We would sneak out at night, buy clove cigarettes, and spend hours at the river or in the woods, talking and making mischief. We made rope swings over rivers, camped out in trucks, played in bands, and stole campaign signs of the other guy when my dad was running for office. (I don't recommend that last one; it got us into *a lot* of trouble.)

There was nothing particularly unique about any of that. Lots of people cut up, and there's nothing particularly special about friends just because you have fun and get into trouble together. We were normal and deeply flawed. But normal and deeply flawed is where all meaningful friendships start.

What made us special, I think, is that we intermixed into all that typical high school mischief inordinate amounts of time spent together talking. We were learning how to be vulnerable and honest and encouraging. We spent night after night together and talked about our lives and our relationships with God.

honor, though, to be named someone's most cherished person. But this is why I think the term *covenant friend* is more useful. It is a way to name a kind of relationship that is entirely set apart while also acknowledging that we may have many covenant friends.

I could not have named the power of words then. We didn't have the language to call vulnerability and honesty the arts of friendship. We were just a ragtag group of high schoolers, but we were also brothers who were growing in our relationships with God as we grew in our relationships with one another.

A few years into those relationships, my brother Mark and his close friend Christian took to calling our group "the Cast." Because the same cast of characters always showed up.

Again, I had no idea the power that name would give. But we all embraced the name, and that name called us forward. We began to see ourselves as something more than coincidence. We didn't just happen to hang out—we were the Cast. We belonged to one another. We stuck together.

Decades later, the Cast is still the Cast. That's who I live near in Richmond. We have a text chain called "The Cast" where we send an obscene number of communications to one another all day, every day. Most of us are in our thirties and have wives and children and jobs, and yet that seemingly happenstance name has in no small part called us forward into a life of committed friendship.

NAMING RELATIONSHIPS HAS A POWER TO SPARK COMMITMENT THAT NO ONE SHOULD IGNORE. WE SHOULD EMBRACE IT AS ONE OF THE ARTS OF FRIENDSHIP.

There is much more to this story, of course. There are dangers of exclusion in having such a group, something I'll address in chapter 5. There is a chosen geography that really does matter that we'll discuss in chapter 6, and there are habits of scheduling and spiritual disciplines that keep us committed, which I'll talk about in chapters 7 and 10.

But suffice it to say that naming relationships has a power to spark commitment that no one should ignore. We should embrace it as one of the arts of friendship.

But alone, a name is not enough. At some point, you must be specific about commitment.

Promising Covenant Friendship

Ten years ago, when I was still in law school, that group of friends all got together for a winter cabin weekend, which was, at the time, one of our annual traditions. I am tempted to pause here to complain about how that *was* one of our annual traditions before we all started having kids and how we rarely have time anymore. But I'll skip the rant because that future of growing up was, in no small part, what we had gathered to talk about.

We had been doing these kinds of weekends throughout our twenties (they kept doing them while I was in China), and when we gathered that winter, there had been a lot of emails and discussion about the future and what that would look like for us.

I was in law school at the time. We had just had our first son, Whit, and my wife was pregnant with our second. I was about to graduate and begin work at a large law firm. I *knew* my life was about to change. I knew that these friendships had carried us to incredible places through our twenties. But I didn't know what was going to happen after, in our thirties.

As a man prone to the written word, I did what I felt was right: I wrote a letter. As a man prone to making awkward gestures, I did another thing I felt was right: I asked if I could read it to them. Being good friends who bear with my eccentricities, they tolerated it. Here, in part, is what it said:

We are still young, but we have done something remarkable already. We have stayed together.

I think where we find ourselves is extremely significant. Significant because the next seven years, I think, are going to be final in a way that the last seven have not. In the next seven years every one of us will be in our thirties, some nearing forty. We are already starting marriages, families, careers, and settling into cities. In the next seven years those things are going to become more and more entrenched. The concrete we're pouring into the habits of our lives is going to dry, and we are going to become the kind of people that we're going to be for a long, long time.

Let me put it another way. The college years and the early twenties lend themselves to a kind of emotional radicalness where you actually can and do completely shift your habits, and we become new people. That window, however, is likely closing. Thus, I think now is the time to consider seriously what kinds of people we are becoming. We have a good start, but I think the next seven years will be far more determinative of what kinds of friends we will be in the long run. The next seven years will show: Will we have the kind of friendships that sustain us through rocky years in marriage? Maybe more important, will we have the kind of friendships that sustain us through the difficulties of not being married yet? Will we have the kind of friends who live as examples to one another's kids? Will we be the kind of friends who support one another finan-cially if a job or business falls through or support one another emotionally if we hit dead ends in our careers? Will we be the kind of friends who won't ignore and won't let one another get into bad emotional, physical, sexual, or financial habits?

I think the summary of what I'm longing for, the reasons why I decided to write all this down, is I see the beginnings of a covenant between us. And I see the possibility of covenant relationships forming in the long run. And I want to name the goodness, to give words to what the Lord is doing among us. I want to call one another not simply by what we are but by what we are hoping to become. I think that might be "covenant friends." I leave whatever form it takes to you, but what I hope is that we begin to think and talk of one another in these terms, in terms of covenant relationships, where we acknowledge that the Lord is binding us together in ways that we don't have the option to separate.

In conclusion, I think our next seven years may be our most important, and I want us to consider pushing into those years consciously, as covenant friends. It might go a long way toward what I hope for as our end. This is what I imagine: that in the long run we will look at one another and say, "I have a lot of friends, but none like you."

This was a tremendously significant moment for me because I had never named the future in that way. I had never thought before about what it would mean to reflect our commitment to one another in words. This letter was the first time I found those words. And writing it changed the way that I thought about my friends.

I think it changed the way we all thought about our relationships. We experienced the divine power of naming friendships and making commitments.

Since that letter was written, the concrete of our lives does indeed seem to have set. While I mourn not having cabin weekends every year, we have still had a few. And while I mourn not being able to drop everything and see anyone at all hours of the night to talk, we still have plenty of grand, long evenings. This is in no small part, as I mentioned, because we have all decided to live in the same city (something I'll address in chapter 6). But living in the same city is not the main thing that keeps us together.

We work at covenant. Our friends' kids call us uncles. We're messy like family. It has not been easy. We have seen friends leave. We have seen marriages fail. We have seen addictions get the better of us, and we have seen emotional collapses. We have counseled one another through lost children and lost parents. We are normal people who get banged up by the world. But we are also, thanks to the grace of God, still friends.

I believe that is not because of random happenstance or good fortune. It is not common history or inherited privilege. It's also not the luck of having old friends—sometimes that kind of person is the hardest to get along with. Longevity of relationship by itself, I believe, has little to do with real friendship.

It is the fruit of covenant given through the grace of God that makes this different. It is what happens when you make a promise and do the hard work of sticking to it.

We have so much of life still before us. And we will see more tragedies and more struggles in the days to come than we have seen in the days past, I'm sure.

But we are now measuring our friendships in decades, not years. And I am not only thankful for it but also proud of my friends.

I am proud to have them. Because the unknown future is a scary thing, and covenanting is too. But God works beautiful things through promises. So make them with friends.

Covenant Friendship Is Not Marriage

Before we go on, let me draw an important distinction. Covenant friendship is not marriage.

As you can see from the table, covenant friendship can be distinguished in important ways both from marriage and from more casual forms of relationship.

In distinguishing from marriage, covenant friendship may be intimate in that we are absorbed in understanding a person

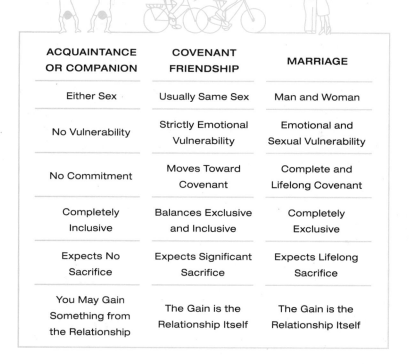

ACQUAINTANCE OR COMPANION	COVENANT FRIENDSHIP	MARRIAGE
Either Sex	Usually Same Sex	Man and Woman
No Vulnerability	Strictly Emotional Vulnerability	Emotional and Sexual Vulnerability
No Commitment	Moves Toward Covenant	Complete and Lifelong Covenant
Completely Inclusive	Balances Exclusive and Inclusive	Completely Exclusive
Expects No Sacrifice	Expects Significant Sacrifice	Expects Lifelong Sacrifice
You May Gain Something from the Relationship	The Gain is the Relationship Itself	The Gain is the Relationship Itself

and having them understand us back. But that is a matter of relational, not physical, intimacy.

Romantic love drives toward physical intimacy, which necessarily means the disclosure of bodies. Friendship drives toward relational intimacy, which necessarily means the disclosure of true selves. Marriage, of course, will have both of these. But friendships will have only the latter.

That doesn't make friendship less valuable; it actually makes it more universal. Not everyone will be married, but everyone should look for two or three covenant friends.

Further, while a healthy marriage will be an example of covenant friendship, I firmly believe everyone married needs covenant friendships outside of their marriages. And of course, if you're single, you're not a second-class citizen of the kingdom. A powerful and historic form of relational intimacy called friendship is available to you right now.

So covenant friendship is not marriage, but it is not mere companionship either. Because our modern definition of friendship is so impoverished, let me try to draw a few key distinctions. People who went before us had words for this. Aristotle is famous for claiming that a life without friendship is not worth living,[9] but he is also famous for distinguishing that having a network you use or an acquaintance you enjoy is far different from having a friend you are bound to in the love of *phileos*.[10]

9. "For friendship is a certain virtue or is accompanied by virtue; and, further, it is most necessary with a view to life: without friends, no one would choose to live, even if he possessed all other goods; and indeed those who are wealthy or have acquired political offices and power seem to be in need of friends most of all" (Aristotle, *The Nicomachean Ethics*, bk. 8, canto 1, trans. Robert C. Bartlett and Susan D. Collins [Chicago: University of Chicago Press, 2011], 163.)

10. One of the reasons we have lost the luster of the word *friendship* is that it used to be one of the versions of the words for love. There was *agape*, about the unconditional love of

Our problem is that the more we talk about love, vulnerability, and promise keeping in friendship, the more we read sexuality into the relationship, which is a mistake. We can be passionate and committed in friendships without being sexual, and this is essential relational ground our modern minds must recover.

Throughout human history, people have thought of a true friend with much of the romance that we might apply to a lover. A true friend is someone you are captivated by. Someone whom you would stand for and who would stand for you. Someone you would not leave.[11] They are there for you.[12] They make you better.[13] They tell you things you don't want to hear but need to.[14] Doesn't this sound like the faithfulness of either a lover or a family member?[15] That's because it is!

This is why when you read the letters of people who lived before us (and note, this is very recent history), their romantic devotion to their friends is almost startling. It may be incomprehensible to us who now (mistakenly) categorize all affection for another person as erotic love; but we are the strange ones! We are the outliers in human history.[16] When we read of

God—a spiritual desire. There was *eros*, about romance—a sexual desire. There was *caritas*, about the love of fellow humans—a desire you ought to have (we pronounce this now as *charity*). But among these there was also *phileos*, about the love we have for our friends.

11. "One who has unreliable friends soon comes to ruin, but there is a friend who sticks closer than a brother" (Prov. 18:24).

12. "A friend is always loyal, and a brother is born to help in time of need" (Prov. 17:17 NLT).

13. "As iron sharpens iron, so a person sharpens his friend" (Prov. 27:17 NET).

14. "Wounds from a friend can be trusted, but an enemy multiplies kisses" (Prov. 27:6).

15. "Never abandon a friend—either yours or your father's. When disaster strikes, you won't have to ask your brother for assistance. It's better to go to a neighbor than to a brother who lives far away" (Prov. 27:10 NLT).

16. "It has actually become necessary in our time to rebut the theory that every firm and serious friendship is really homosexual [even when there is no evidence of such]. . . . A belief in invisible cats perhaps cannot be logically disproved, but it tells us a great deal about those who hold it. Those who cannot conceive Friendship as a substantive love but

men[17] (or women[18]) who were inspired to poetry and devotion toward same-sex affection and assume they must have "really" been same-sex attracted but society just was not progressive enough to allow it, we are strikingly arrogant in our thinking that we know more about their desires than they did; we are also impoverished in our imagination of friendship.[19] An old Chinese proverb goes something like this: "A frog in a well cannot discuss the ocean, because he is limited by the size of his well." It would do us good to come out of our modern well and gaze on the vast relational horizon friendship has to offer.

There is a category of deep, platonic love for same-sex friends that we moderns have overlooked. Naming covenant friendship is one way to recover that depth of friendship we have lost.

only as a disguise or elaboration of Eros betray the fact that they have never had a Friend." (Lewis, "Friendship," in *The Four Loves* (San Francisco: HarperOne, 2017], 76–77.)

17. Consider Jonathan and David's exchange before their parting: "David got up from the south side of the stone and bowed down before Jonathan three times, with his face to the ground. Then they kissed each other and wept together—but David wept the most" (1 Sam. 20:41). Consider also the words Abraham Lincoln famously wrote to his friend Joshua Speed: "You know my desire to befriend you is everlasting, that I will never cease, while I know how to do any thing." (Doris Kearns Goodwin, *Team of Rivals* [2005; repr., New York: Simon and Schuster, 2006], 58.)

18. "Don't urge me to leave you or to turn back from you. Where you go I will go, and where you stay I will stay. Your people will be my people and your God my God. Where you die I will die, and there I will be buried. May the LORD deal with me, be it ever so severely, if even death separates you and me" (Ruth 1:16–17). Note that the familial bond between Ruth and Naomi had been broken, and typically Ruth would have returned to her family, which is what makes this statement on friendship remarkable. Consider also the words of Charlotte Brontë to her friend Ellen Nussey: "Why are we to be divided? Surely, Ellen, it must be because we are in danger of loving each other too well—in losing sight of the Creator in idolatry of the creature" (Alexander Nehamas, *On Friendship* [New York: Basic Books, 2016], 5).

19. "Figuring out what these romantic friendships meant to people living in the eighteenth century involves setting aside the modern assumptions about love between members of the same sex. . . . [People today] assume that expressions of loving devotion must imply a desire for sexual intimacy, or, to put it another way, that people who are in love with one another must want to have sex. . . . Yet however compelling our own models and categories may seem to us, they will not necessarily enable us to see the world as people living in the past saw it." (Richard Godbeer, *The Overflowing of Friendship: Love between Men and the Creation of the American Republic* [Baltimore: Johns Hopkins University Press, 2009], 2–3.)

The art of living into covenant may seem like a grand gesture, but I think it depends on much smaller habits that occur in little, but nonetheless powerful, rhythms in our relationships. Here are some thoughts on that, big and small.

Move toward a Few Covenant Friends

My examples may lead you to believe that you need lifelong friendships to find covenant friends. But remember, stories are windows to look through, not pictures to look at. My hope here is to get you to imagine the possibility of covenant friendships, not imitate mine.

Please hear me clearly: you do not need decades-old high school friendships to have covenant friends. Many of mine are not. Neither do you need a lot of covenant friendships. Even one or two will do. You also do not need to be young to start. Covenant friendship is much more a product of vulnerability than time. This means you can start right now, no matter how old you are and no matter where you are.

Remember, friendship is not marriage, and many friendships will not be conceived of as lifelong commitments. So you do not need to try to turn every relationship you have into a covenant friendship. Instead, you should look at the relationships you have and simply try to move toward the beauty and helpfulness of covenant friendship. This can happen in small and myriad ways. Covenant friendship will not always be the destination you land in, but it can be a direction you move in.

The following table presents some practical ways to move different relationships toward covenant friendship.

The Next Step toward Covenant Friendship

Kind of Friendship		
	LIFELONG FRIENDS WHO LIVE NEARBY	If you have very close friends who live in the same town with you, my suggestion is to consider naming those relationships as covenant friendships to push them deeper. This may happen by conversation, by committing to read this book together and discuss it, or even by writing and signing a covenant (more on that later). But find some way to name the future you want to pursue together.
	THOSE YOU RARELY SEE OR LIVE FAR FROM	You may have friends you are very close to but rarely see. Perhaps this is a life stage, or perhaps you live far away. My suggestion in these kinds of relationships is to move toward covenant by naming a routine. This could be a monthly phone call or a seasonal gathering. But holding to a ritual of friendship can move you toward a covenant friendship even when it happens only once in a while. This is true of some of my covenant friends, such as Barrett. Now our relationship subsists mainly on a quarterly hangout. We call it our quarterly cocktail. But even though Barrett and I get together only a couple of times a year, we have found that a lightning bolt of friendship comes with the commitment to be honest and intentional , even when it's occasional.
	THOSE WHO DON'T FOLLOW JESUS	You may have close friends who do not know Jesus. I pray you do. I often have people ask me, "Can these, too, be covenant friendships?" My answer is a joyful yes. With those friends, despite not sharing your most important thing in common—Jesus—there is nonetheless tremendous enjoyment, mutual respect, brotherhood, sisterhood, or shared history. The fact that they do not follow Jesus should not prevent you from "fully knowing and loving anyway." "Fully knowing" is a continual opportunity for natural and organic evangelism (more on that in chapter 5). But even without such words, you get the opportunity to "be Christ"

(continued)

The Next Step toward Covenant Friendship

Kind of Friendship		
	THOSE WHO DON'T FOLLOW JESUS	to someone who doesn't know him. Further, these friends also hold you and bear the gift of Christ to you even if they don't know the name of the gift they bring.

Therefore, my suggestion is to give them the gift of commitment by naming the friendship. Even if this is just a conversation where you say out loud how they have been like Christ to you, such naming could be an incredible blessing to them, and perhaps, you can pray, a breadcrumb along the path of their realizing that Christ is at the root of all friendship even for those who don't know him yet. |
| | **PEOPLE YOU NO LONGER SEE** | There are also friends with whom you walked for some time as covenant friends but no longer see. This may be because of a move or because of a change in life stage or something else entirely. Simply because you no longer see such a friend does not mean that the friendship has failed. Cherishing a past friendship that you no longer live into may be a sign that the friendship served you well and moved you to the next place of life.

While it is sad to see a covenant friendship move into the past, you do not have to feel shame or guilt as if you did anything wrong. When we lose contact with a covenant friend, we can acknowledge our limitations as human beings and cherish the past. You will see them again and have plenty of evenings to savor together in the kingdom to come. (More on leaving friendships in chap. 4.)

Consider calling or visiting or writing that person to name the friendship they gave you and to thank and encourage them for it. This was my goal in the conversation with Ken I wrote about in chapter 2, and this kind of naming could be an incredible Ebenezer in your relationship, even if there is little chance you'll be spending regular time together in the future. |
| | **FAMILY MEMBERS** | Your family is paradoxically both the easiest and the hardest place to pursue covenant friendships.

The easy may be obvious. There are, sometimes, gifts of family members. Siblings you grew up with who know you |

(continued)

Kind of Friendship

FAMILY MEMBERS

inside and out and you can share anything with. A brother or a sister who is also your best friend and always will be. These gifts may be rare, but they are real, and they are, in some ways, a shining model of covenant friendship.

But usually, making friends out of family is very difficult. This is important to reiterate. It is not longevity, or proximity, that is the hallmark of friendship. If that were true, our siblings and parents and spouses would always be our best friends. Instead, it is often hardest to enter into real friendship with family members. Quantity and history of time together can be baggage as much as it is a gift. This suggests that with family members, there still may be a lot of work to do to move toward real vulnerability and really loving one another despite all your flaws (which are usually on display with family).

If you have a family member with whom you want to move toward covenant friendship, consider having one of those hard, watershed conversations where you try to be vulnerable about what you long for with them. Do not tell them what they need to do differently but rather what you hope for in that relationship. Start the vulnerability. Often we have the commitment part with family members, but we lack the true vulnerability part.

CHURCH COMMUNITIES

My working assumption is that church communities and covenant friendships are interwoven. Like a building constructed with strong bars of steel, I believe covenant friendships are uniquely supportive of the larger church community. They are distinct from the whole but an integral part of the whole. We should be mindful of how church programs can funnel people into smaller gatherings that enable the possibility of covenant friendships. No church program can create covenant friendships for you, but you can serve your church mightily by being the kind of person who seeks covenant friendships within the community you already have.

(continued)

The Next Step toward Covenant Friendship

WHEN YOU'RE JUST NOT SURE

There may be plenty of friendships in your life that don't fit any of the previous categories. You're not sure where they're headed. That is fine. Relationships usually defy categorization. My suggestion is to pick one that you are encouraged by and make a gesture of covenant. Perhaps you give a gift that cannot be used until the future—a bottle of wine to be opened later or tickets to a concert a year from now. Maybe you suggest a family vacation together or plan a party together. Gestures of covenant, no matter how small, may change things far more than you think.

Written Covenants

Many people ask me whether a written covenant is a good idea for friends. As a contract lawyer who believes deeply in the power of the written word, you may be surprised to hear that writing a covenant for friendship is not necessarily my top recommendation. If you feel it fits your situation, I am all for it and encourage you to try it. But I have found that most people find the smaller gestures of covenant more sincere, more encouraging, and more do-able.

My friends and I did write a covenant of friendship together at one point. You can take a look at it in the appendix at the back of the book and see whether you gain anything from it. The act of writing and discussing it sparked a lot of good conversation and thought. But to be honest, no one was terribly interested in signing or framing it, and I think that is normal and speaks to the nature of covenant friendships. They are distinct from life-long covenants like marriage. And yet we still desperately need a way to elevate them far above the disposable nature of typical modern relationships. So whether it's in writing or in gestures, I encourage you to take the next step in the direction of covenant, whatever that is.

Make the First Move

If you are reading this and starting to feel lonely because you do not have friendships like this and cannot imagine finding them, let me take a moment to comfort you and exhort you. First, remember, you are normal. We are all in the current of loneliness, and while it may not be comforting, it is still true: most people feel the way you do.

The upside of this is that, like at a high school dance, most of us are sitting around waiting to be asked. When you get the bravery to be the one to ask, you'll find everyone else has been dying to say yes.

So let me exhort you out of self-pity and into awkward initiation. Ask someone in your life to move into a deeper kind of friendship. It will be awkward, but it will also change both of your lives.

Waiting for the Future

In the back of my top dresser drawer sits that bottle with 2035 written on the top. Every few months I check on it, not because I'm worried it will go anywhere but because I want to think for a minute about sitting down and feeling old and still being friends.

It is hard to describe the kind of comfort this can bring. Knowing that you have friends who will be there no matter what—or who at least will try—is truly a different way of seeing the future.

Christians do not know the future, but we rest in peace

because we know the one who has secured our future. We know the fundamental fact of the world is that God keeps his promises, and he has promised to love us—come what may. This is the real island in the ocean of life. This is the only real calm in the storm.

Because even in covenant friendships, conflict and confusion and pain are still real. If covenant and commitment are the ways we imitate God to deal with the uncertain future, forgiveness allows us to imitate God to deal with the past. And that, too, is an art of friendship. So let's talk about that next.

CHAPTER 4

Forgiveness

The Art of Failure and the
Habit of Forgiving

A while back I opened a voice mail on my phone that I had been avoiding for two weeks because I was afraid of what was in it.

Finally, at 9:00 p.m. on a drive to a friend's birthday party, I decided to face my fears and open it. I was thirty seconds in when I heard the words, "I just wanted to apologize for what happened."

I pulled over to the side of the road, and I wept. Real friendship can hurt. A lot.

J. C. Ryle once wrote that friendship "halves our troubles and doubles our joys."[1] Which rings true. But the half of trouble is still real trouble. There is a shadow side to friendship.

No one can hurt us more than our friends can. Which means that you cannot practice real friendship without practicing real forgiveness. Constantly.

If covenant is the way we plan for the future, forgiveness is the way we deal with the past.[2]

---

1. J. C. Ryle, "The Best Friend," chap. 14 in *Practical Religion: Being Plain Papers on the Daily Duties, Experience, Dangers, and Privileges of Professing Christians*, 4th ed. (London: National Protestant Church Union, 1900; repr., Kerry, Ireland: CrossReach Publications, 2019).

2. "The philosopher Hannah Arendt pointed out that if forgiveness is the way we exercise our God-likeness over the past, then promising is the way we bear out the image of God on the future." (Lewis B. Smedes, "Controlling the Unpredictable—The Power of Promising," *Christianity Today*, December 1, 2022, www.christianitytoday .com/ct/2002/decemberweb-only/12-16-56.0.html. Smedes is most likely referencing Arendt's thoughts as expressed in her book *The Human Condition* [Chicago: University of Chicago Press, 1958].)

Getting Comfortable with the Reality of Flawed Friends

Most modern friendships last only until the first conflict. Like plastic cups, we toss them out and just grab new ones. But why would we expect deep relationships without deep conflict?

Here is the thing about your friends: they are sinners. Here is the thing about you as a friend: you are too.

This means all of our friendships and communities have the same active ingredient: sinful people like us. So we should not be surprised in the least that we hurt one another. Often deeply. On the contrary, we should expect to be hurt by our friends.

This is, at first, counterintuitive. It is easy to get caught up in romanticized visions of friends who have no conflict, share only laughter, aren't bogged down with the ordinary pains of life, and are deeply grateful for one another's commitment.

The problem with that vision is that it's a total lie.

To be friends with sinners is our only option. You should expect to be friends with people who are downright selfish, who don't care for you exactly the way you hoped, who miss opportunities, and who let you down. The question is, What do we do with the painful reality that friendship hurts?

We will answer that question momentarily, but to ignore the question is to entertain a false vision of friendship without conflict. A false vision of friendship (like a false vision of marriage or a false vision of church community) is the greatest enemy to the real thing.

Bonhoeffer saw this when he wrote *Life Together*. In a work that is otherwise soaring with encouragement and hopefulness, his passages on false visions of community are the strongest rebukes in the whole text. "Innumerable times a whole community has broken down because it had sprung from a wish dream. The serious Christian, set down for the first time in a Christian community, is likely to bring with him a very definite idea of what Christian life together should be and to try to realize it. But God's grace speedily shatters such dreams."[3]

I love that Bonhoeffer sees the shattering of our false visions as a grace.

TO BE FRIENDS WITH SINNERS IS OUR ONLY OPTION.

He is right. We often forget that it is our failures that God uses as the means for encountering grace. On hearing the voice of God in his own struggle, Paul writes, "'My grace is sufficient for you, for my power is made perfect in weakness.' Therefore I will boast all the more gladly about my weaknesses, so that Christ's power may rest on me."[4]

That logic of grace does not change on a communal level.

You may think that conflict with your friends is the barrier to deeper friendship. But that is true only if you do not practice forgiveness.

With forgiveness, conflict in friendship is the doorway to communal grace.

---

3. Dietrich Bonhoeffer, *Life Together: The Classic Exploration of Christian Community*, trans. John W. Doberstein (New York: HarperSanFrancisco, 1978), 26. To continue the quote: "Just as surely as God desires to lead us to a knowledge of genuine Christian fellowship, so surely must we be overwhelmed by a great disillusionment with others, with Christians in general, and, if we are fortunate, with ourselves. By sheer grace, God will not permit us to live even for a brief period in a dream world. He does not abandon us to those rapturous experiences and lofty moods that come over us like a dream. God is not a God of the emotions but the God of truth." (Ibid., 26–27.)
4. 2 Corinthians 12:9.

Practicing Forgiveness

The reasons to forgive are eminently practical. Relationships cannot exist without forgiveness. Either we forgive or we fall apart; there is no middle ground.

Given that all good friends will eventually hurt you, if you do not practice forgiveness, you will either be stuck in a cycle of endless resentment or never have a true friendship at all. In a moment that has elevated the spirit of cancel culture and downplayed the beauty of forgiveness, it is no surprise that so many are drifting into the loneliness of resentment. Here again we must swim against the current if we are to have friendships at all.

But even more than practical, forgiveness is profound. Here is the strange reversal: forgiveness is for us as much as it is for our friends who hurt us. In his parable of the unmerciful servant, Jesus told of a man whose debt was mercifully forgiven, but then the man went on to mercilessly demand repayment from others.[5] The way he treated others showed that the servant didn't understand what had happened to him.

The most important reason we forgive others is to reexperience the way Jesus has forgiven us. We learn it by practicing it.

Importantly, our forgiveness is not predicated on our friends' apologies. We don't forgive one another because of how good the apologies are, we forgive one another because Christ has forgiven us.[6]

In practice, this does not mean pretending your friends did not hurt you but rather first acknowledging that they did. Then, instead of inflicting pain to make them pay, you bear the burden

5. Matthew 18:21–35.
6. Ephesians 4:32.

of the pain. This is the logic of our salvation: Christ bore our burden so we wouldn't have to. It is also how friendships work.[7]

I recently had a difficult conversation with a friend I needed to forgive. It began with a text saying, "Can we talk?" I recommend that. If there is someone in your life you need to forgive, then initiate with them. What happened next was we set aside an evening to be face-to-face and say the things we were hurt by. Unsurprisingly, there were mutual errors, and I had to apologize too. Also unsurprisingly, I didn't get the perfect apology I craved. Yet remarkably, we left in forgiveness, with imperfect apologies accepted, and continue to work toward deeper friendship.

Without the practice of forgiveness, I know we would both still be burning in anger, incessantly turning over in our heads the things that were said, consumed by perceived slights. That is who we become without forgiveness. But because of the grace of Jesus for us, this conflict became the doorway to deeper grace. This friend and I have found a second chance *and* a more tender friendship.

Practicing Apology

If you are like me, more often than not you are the one who needs to ask for forgiveness. And as awkward as it can be, I am now convinced of this truth: I have often regretted not apologizing, but I have never regretted apologizing.

Wanting to apologize is one thing, but practicing it is something else entirely.

I recall a conversation that forever changed how I apologize.

---

7. We will talk more about when it is healthy to leave a friendship, or what to do when someone is unhealthy and hurting others, but it does not change the primacy of forgiveness. Even in friendships that have to end, forgiveness should be extended first.

I was sitting at a lunch table in the back of a Chinese restaurant with a friend as I explained to him the ways I had been acting selfishly and avoiding relationship with him.

I had treated this brother in Christ childishly, meanly, selfishly, and even worse, I had gaslit him by doing these things in a way that made it seem like he had the problem, not me. I was awful. Eventually (with the help of some other friends' rebuke!) I came to see it. It took me weeks, but I finally could admit that I needed to apologize. So I asked him to lunch.

I explained what I felt I had done and said, "I'm sorry." It came out stone cold, with no emotion.

"It's fine, man, I get it. I forgive you," he said, I think because he didn't know what else to say.

In theory, we could have been done there. Papered some correct words over the wound of emotions and called it a success. But I remember sitting there thinking that this wasn't right. Perhaps I hadn't said enough. So I continued:

"No, I'm actually really sorry. What I did was mean."

He was quiet.

Then, half because it didn't seem to be getting through and half (I believe now) because of a prompting of the Holy Spirit, I just started repeating, "I'm sorry."

My friend looked at me across the table as I said it again and again and again, until, after the sixth or seventh time, I began to cry and finally felt like I was saying something true.

"I'm so sorry," I ended.

That's when he teared up, too, and forgave me, and for a moment, at a lunch table in a small Chinese restaurant, two weeping men found confession, forgiveness, and reconciliation.

Sometimes you need words to lead your heart. So practice as

often as you need to, and say sorry until you mean it, but don't avoid the pain. You will never regret apologizing.

The Gift of Grace in Being Friends with Sinners

Practicing the habits of apology and forgiveness means taking a lifetime of moments that would otherwise be the undoing of relationship and turning them into entry points for deeper relationship.

Put otherwise, our failures do not have to be roadblocks to friendship, they can become the building blocks of it. Grace, as it turns out, is a much sturdier foundation for relationship than perfection. Grace means that the failures of friends can be the cause of our coming together, not the cause of our falling apart. Here are four ways that grace should change the way you practice friendship:

1. Grace Frees

First, grace is freeing. When forgiveness is an art of friendship, you and your friends can bring the real versions of yourselves. One hundred percent of the time, that is a flawed person. There is no version of yourself that you can bring except the deeply flawed one that you actually are. Likewise, there is no version of your friend that you can expect except the deeply flawed one that he or she actually is.

2. Grace Reforms Expectations

Second, grace delivers you from the burden of unhealthy expectations of others. "True friendships do not demand perfection."[8]

8. David Benner, *Sacred Companions: The Gift of Spiritual Friendship Direction* (Downers Grove, IL: InterVarsity Press, 2002), 82.

If you seem to be constantly disappointed with your friends, the first thing to do is not to look for new ones or wonder why they are such idiots who don't seem to understand relationships. The first thing to do is examine *your* expectations of relationships. Because it is very possible that our bitterness about the relationships around us speaks more to our pride than their flaws.

3. Grace Allows Us to Practice Friendship

Third, grace allows us to "practice" friendship in the truest sense of the word. Without forgiveness, we live in a world that demands perfection, and friendship does not exist in that world. But when we live in a world that instead offers grace, friendships can finally bloom.

This is particularly true of covenant friendship. Consider what we've talked about up until now: to be real friends with someone is to put your whole emotional life—and more—at risk. When you are vulnerable about your secrets and honest about your fragile hopes, you essentially give a friend the weapons with which to wound you. Friends are already like bulls wandering into the delicate china shops of one another's lives— add promising, and it is like asking the bull to live there. It all but guarantees that something will go wrong and someone will get hurt. Probably really hurt. Without forgiveness, we will never even risk the pain of covenant friendship. But with forgiveness, we are free to be hurt and try again.

This may not be the easy life, but it is the good life.[9] If you're not willing to get hurt, you're not willing to have

9. "A good life [is] forged from precisely the things that make it hard." (Robert Waldinger and Marc Schulz, *The Good Life: Lessons from the World's Longest Scientific Study of Happiness* [New York: Simon and Schuster, 2022], 3.)

relationships. If you want to stay safe, never be hurt again, and protect yourself from the serious and inevitable pain of relationships, then you need to stay out of friendships. Especially covenant friendships—because these friendships have enough time and history and expectation and hope to really hurt us. No one can hurt us like the ones we love most and love longest.

IF YOU'RE NOT WILLING TO GET HURT, YOU'RE NOT WILLING TO HAVE RELATIONSHIPS.

But remaining safe from the pain and conflict of relationships also means remaining hard, or remaining bitter, and always remaining in the restless wandering of loneliness. If Aristotle is right that a life without friendship isn't worth living, that means a life without pain and frustration is not worth living either.

Friendship may make us live longer, but it does so in the same way exercising does. By hurting you in the right way. Friendship is the exercise of the heart. Over time our hearts grow bigger, stronger, and more able to love more people.

4. Grace Forms Us into the Image of Christ

Finally and most important, grace is how friendships form us into the image of Christ. This cannot be overstated.

Consider the friend that Jesus was. He was, famously, the "friend of sinners." What do you suppose it was like for him when he sat down in rooms of liars, cheats, and prostitutes like us? Do you think they suddenly behaved? Do you think some of them didn't mock him? Do you think some of them didn't ignore him and talk only to the one they thought they could get in bed with that night?

But the very character of Jesus is to be drawn to those who

would hurt him and push him away. Our calling in friendship is the same.

Friendship hurts. And like most fundamental truths, this one may be as obvious as it is overlooked.

We are not called to friendship to simplify our lives, we're called to friendship to sanctify our lives. And this necessarily means the friction and pain of iron sharpening iron.[10] This friction of friendship is a gift, not a curse! Iron does not sharpen iron without a great deal of noise, heat, and colliding. You will know a true friend by such noise and heat and, yes, even the pain of colliding.

If it were the opposite, Jesus never would have invited suffering into the Trinity by coming to be with us. But in the incarnation, Jesus showed us that the way to divine friendship is not around pain, but through it.

If you want to pursue happiness, then stick with companions. People who like the same things you do. And make sure to leave them whenever things start to turn toward real friendship.

But if you want to pursue holiness, then find covenant friends and stick around long enough to get hurt, forgive, and get hurt and forgive again. In the pursuit of happiness, you'll find neither happiness nor holiness. In the pursuit of holiness, you'll find both.

So yes, this kind of friendship involves pain. But we imitate Christ in our friendships by facing that pain.

Being like Christ means being a friend like Christ. So it is our call, too, to go to people who are broken up, worn down, half put together, and entirely flawed and act out the ethic of

---

10. Proverbs 27:17.

A FRIEND IS SOMEONE WHO KNOWS YOU FULLY AND LOVES YOU ANYWAY.

Christ: "You are broken, and that means I'll get hurt, but I'm sticking around to love you anyway."

On Losing and Leaving Friendships

Does the art of forgiveness mean we should never lose or leave a friendship? The answer is no. Unlike the way we approach marriage, we should expect to lose and leave some friendships. Though both are sad, both are also a part of life on this side of the kingdom. In both cases, the hope of the kingdom to come helps us navigate the difficulty and pain of loss and leaving.

Losing Friendships Is Inevitable

"The art of losing isn't hard to master."[11] So writes Elizabeth Bishop in a poem about the inevitability of loss in life.

To be human is to lose things. We lose keys and loved ones, we forget languages we once learned and names we just learned, we move on to new jobs and into new phases, we look at old pictures of ourselves and try to remember who we used to be. We look at the friends next to us in those pictures and wonder what happened.

This is certainly true in my life.

I've lost some friends because of distance. These are friends I miss dearly and still talk to once in a while, but the reality is that our lives and our callings don't allow for the relationships we once had. One friend, for example, took a humanitarian relief job in the Middle East. Another pastored a church in the Midwest. One found a wife in England. I still count these people

11. Elizabeth Bishop, "One Art," in *The Complete Poems: 1927–1979* (New York: Farrar, Straus and Giroux, 1983), 178.

as friends, even covenant friends in a real sense—we could probably catch up on a deep level at any time. But I don't think any of us hold guilt or a grudge that we haven't caught up in years and probably won't.

In this kind of loss, it is appropriate and even right to mourn the limits of being human. Part of what it means not to be God is that we are not omnipresent. We are located in one place and time, and the reality is that we cannot—and should not—try to hold on to every friendship for our whole lives. To do so would be a kind of idol, a rebellion against the way God made us. But we can mourn the loss.

Some relationships may be lost to something more than distance. Perhaps you didn't call enough or someone didn't make time. Perhaps there was no major conflict but just a growing distance that seemed to suggest you were both moving into a new phase of life.

This is also a real kind of loss. I assume you, like me, could spend all day analyzing these. *Should I have reached out more? Why didn't they make time?* But I encourage us both to let it rest.

Part of the art of forgiveness is turning your head from the "what if" of the past to the "what will" of the future. This means forgiving yourself and others for the gray, ambiguous things we can't quite name that went wrong.

Of course this is painful. Elizabeth Bishop was a little too right. The art of losing isn't hard to master. No one needs to teach us. We're already pretty good at it.

But we can be sad without being ashamed. Friendships are not marriages. You can lose a lot of them and still be really healthy. Because even in loss, we can take heart in the kingdom to come. There will be plenty of evenings by the fire, laughing and catching up, and talking with great hope about all that lies ahead.

Leaving Friendships Is Complicated

Leaving friendships is different. Where losing friendships is a result of being human, leaving friendships is much more a product of our sin and fallenness.

The painful truth is that we will lose some friends to sin. And as painful as it may seem, sometimes it is more right to leave a friendship than to fight for it.

Some friends cling to an addiction or fall to mental illness and refuse to get help. Some make choices that harm you and others or decide that they'd rather keep moving around to new communities than settle down in a real community and face their issues. Some decide that a life of affairs and unfettered sex is what will finally make them happy. Some seem to lose their faith despite their best efforts.

Some may be a mix of all of these things. I've experienced each of those examples, and these friendships were painful to leave. But at some point, in each case, I had to face the humbling reality that I could not fix them.

While I hope for reconciliation in each of them, while I try to make a practice to pray for these friends when they come to mind, and while I refuse to speak ill of them, for the time, these are friends I have left or let leave.

Though I truly believe with all my heart, mind, and strength that our call as friends is to be like Christ in the lives of others, we are still not Jesus. We are far from it. We are shards of glass, with all the rough edges, and often we hurt as much as we help. At the end of the day, friends do save one another from all kinds of evil. A friend is faithful to the end.[12] But we don't ultimately deliver one another. Only Jesus can do that. And there are relationships that we can't save.

This book is about fighting for a life of friendship. But it is not necessarily about fighting for the life of each and every friendship on its own.

There are no clear lines, no three-step processes, and no comfortable ways to deal with this shadow side of friendship. If it feels incredibly painful and confusing, it's because it is.

Friends fail. We always will. Friends leave you. Sometimes for bad reasons. The pain is immense. It should be. It is right to lament. But it is also, sometimes, right to leave or let them leave.

> THIS BOOK IS ABOUT FIGHTING FOR A LIFE OF FRIENDSHIP. BUT IT IS NOT NECESSARILY ABOUT FIGHTING FOR THE LIFE OF EACH AND EVERY FRIENDSHIP ON ITS OWN.

Forgive them, always. Forget them, never. But do not try to cling to every gift you have been given.

Here are some blurry lines of wisdom that may be helpful:

First, do not leave a friendship without being honest. Perhaps their addiction is driving them away from everyone. Perhaps their unhealthy relationship (romantic or otherwise) is pulling them away from community. Perhaps their scattered pattern of life makes it impossible to stay in community. Perhaps there's something else, but remember the art of honesty. You cannot and should not try to control people, but you can and should have a

---

12. "A friend loves at all times, and a brother is born for a time of adversity" (Prov. 17:17).

hard conversation. Sometimes in person, sometimes maybe by a letter. Some circumstances merit an intervention. In some cases you should recommend professional or pastoral counseling. Only wisdom, prayer, and the counsel of friends can help you know which approach is right.

IF:	REMEMBER:
Their hard life circumstances make them less available	Children, a difficult job season, marriage problems, physical suffering, and emotional trauma all will make it very hard for people to be the friends they want to be, but don't leave just because things are hard. Hard life circumstances are the soil of—not the barrier to—friendship. Work through those things.
They say or do something dumb or offensive, online or elsewhere	All of us make horrible mistakes. It is the mark of a Pharisee, not a Christian, to break off ties because someone becomes "immoral." It makes us less like Christ—not more—to distance ourselves because we have discovered a flaw in someone else. If their words or actions are preventing them from friendship, then we may be in the previous category. But if they are just offending your moral sensibilities, don't turn your nose up at another human being. We are all terribly flawed people—but God loves us anyway. So we can too.
Their suffering makes them continually sad to be around	All of us, at some point in our lives, and some of us much more and for much longer than others, encounter suffering that drives us into the dirt. We have a difficult time experiencing joy, depression overwhelms, and we aren't much fun to be around. That is when we need the soft faithfulness of friends more than ever. A true friend will say, "I will walk with you, even though I may have to carry you." Don't mistake the hard seasons of relationship for the end of relationship. Those seasons will make you more loving in the end.

Second, be careful that you don't misinterpret difficulty for unredeemable flaws. For example:

Christ Is Preeminent

Losing and leaving are difficult matters.

I wish I could tell you a tidy end to the story of the voice mail I told you about. I sat with the voice mail for months, too nervous to call back. Until I finally did. And then there was a halting, cautious catch up. Some short but sincere apologies. Now there are plans for a coffee to talk at length, which is something, but there's still a long road to travel.

Like life, this story is not tidy. It probably never will be. That's why we need the art of forgiveness. Sometimes we must let a friendship go. Sometimes friendships are hard but worth it anyway. Only in wisdom and prayer can we tell the difference.

But take comfort that in all this grayness, Christ is preeminent. Sometimes you will say, "I will be like Christ. I will suffer for your good." And you will trust Christ to work in that. This is holy. Sometimes you will have to say, "Only Christ can be Christ," and you will suffer for having to let a friend go and trust Christ to take care of them. This, too, is holy.

In the end, both are acts of faith in Christ and ways that we can let the shape of Christ's work in the world be the shape of our friendships in the world.

Friendship, Forgiveness, and the Kingdom to Come

I have a dear friend whom I have lost. I think of him often.

Sometimes—honestly, quite often—I see him in dreams. When I wake, I sense the dread of conflict and pain. I sense the awkwardness of what used to be. I long to avoid it. At the same time, I so very much want to go back to what our friendship used to be. I miss it. I just don't know how to get there.

Recently I've tried to embrace a practice. Instead of imagining a conversation where we fight over what has been done to each other and I justify my words, I imagine our reunion in the kingdom. I imagine us coming down a road to greet each other. I imagine us shaking hands and laughing. I imagine us walking off and catching up and being delighted that we have all the time in the world to do it.

I imagine this not to ease the pain but to make the truest sense of the pain—because that *is* what we will do one day.

The gift of Jesus' reconciliation is not theoretical. It is not only a psychology to be practiced today. It is a reality that will bear the fruit of reconciliation. I tell myself that. And then let myself be sad and hopeful at the same time, which is not a contradiction.

We can close on that hope of reconciliation in the kingdom to come.

Sin would put an end to every relationship, but the gift of the cross means the possibility of enduring friendships. You have been forgiven much, so you can turn and forgive what friends have done. You have been forgiven much, so you can also forgive yourself for what you have done. We cannot force reconciliation now, but we can always forgive.

Without forgiveness, there is no friendship.

CHAPTER 5

Invitation

The Art of Open Circles and
the Habit of Inclusion

It was my junior year of high school, and Steve and I were about to jump into a friend's convertible to drive downtown to a music store when someone else showed up in the high school parking lot and asked to join. He was a freshman, and we didn't know him that well, but we couldn't think of a polite way to say no. So we said, "Okay. Get in."

It became clear along the way that this new guy had good taste in music and an even better sense of humor, but for most of the ride, we were just confused about how he'd made his way into our car. We didn't even know his name. Regardless, it was clear he wanted a friend.

I look back at us then and think that we were nice to let someone tag along. We weren't jerks. But on the other hand, we had a good thing going, and we didn't really want to open up our friendship to someone new. I don't think we could have verbalized it, but we thought that the way to honor the friendship we had was to protect it. We thought that to keep the circle alive and well we needed to keep it closed.

So we let this guy tag along for a day, but after that it was back to sending signals that "That was it." We weren't really willing to open up our friendship.

That closed-off impulse made us normal human beings. Most of us, in fact, are better at protecting our friendships by keeping others out than we are at growing friendships by letting others in.

The problem is, we are all wrong about that.

Keeping friendships closed is the way to hurt them and others too.

The Open Circle of the Trinity

Being made for people means that we do an incredible thing when we open up our lives to others. We mirror the Trinity and satisfy an innate need that we all have—to be invited into the circle.

The reason human friendship is possible is because of the generous openness of the Trinity.

Dwell on that.

Humans would not exist, much less be endowed with the capacity and the yearning for friendship, except that God in his generosity wanted to invite others into the Trinity.

This is the story of salvation. We were created in the image of the Trinity, and despite our fallenness, Jesus' death and resurrection allows us to become one with God. Literally united with Christ, which is nothing short of a divine invitation to the fellowship of the Trinity. The Christian psychologist and author David Benner puts it well when he reflects on Jesus' words on friendship in John 15: "These words are among the most amazing recorded in Scripture. Jesus, the Christ, the Son of God, invites us into the intimacy of the circle of friendship that exists between him and the Father."[1]

The very direction of God is to invite others in.

---

1. David Benner, *Sacred Companions: The Gift of Spiritual Friendship Direction* (Downers Grove, IL: InterVarsity Press, 2002), 65.

The Awful Distortion of Exclusion

All the best things God made—sex, work, technology, power—have shown us that the better something is, the more capacity it has to break us. And friendship is on this short list of the most wonderful and dangerous things God made.

One of the most awful powers we have is the power to exclude someone from friendship.

Being kept out of relationship is one of the deepest pains you can experience. Sensing that others have friendships that you are not welcome in can hurt in a way that makes you forget all the ones you are welcome in.

What we don't usually realize is that excluding is just as dangerous in the long run for the one doing the excluding as it is for the one being excluded. That ended up being true for me and Steve. Something in me started to decay when I focused more on keeping someone out rather than inviting someone in.

I think about this often when I walk along the James River with my sons. Mere blocks from our house, the James River offers places for paddleboarding, fishing, white-water kayaking, swimming, building campfires on the river rocks, and more. On any given afternoon you can find Richmonders wandering down to the James and exploring the endless gift that is a river running through a city. But these good parts of the river have something essential in common—there is a flow of water. Whether flat water or rapids, as long as there is some current of flow in and flow out, the James teems with wildlife and health and fun. But where the river gets low and strands pools in rocks and eddies along the edges, where the water stops flowing and becomes stagnant, things begin to die, and you certainly don't want to go splashing around and swimming there.

We are more like rivers than we know. When blessing flows in, it is meant to flow out. When we prevent that, we turn good things into dangerous things. Friendship is no different.

When excluding others is a motivating impulse of our friendships, we harm ourselves and those friendships. We become like the stagnant pools of water that slowly kill things.

Usually, we're not slamming relational doors in people's faces. We find other, far more subtle ways to signal that we're not open to new friendship. The subtlety makes it all the more dangerous.

I know because I've done it.

Unfortunately, that's what Steve and I both did. We saw our friendship as something to protect, not something to risk for the sake of an outsider. We were the opposite of Christ and the Trinity. We began to actively find ways to show this new guy that we were doing fine on our own and didn't need any new friends.

I remember that season being hurtful. For everyone.

The hurt for this new guy was obvious: he was just like all of us, a lonely wanderer looking for a way to be known and loved, looking for a friend. We denied him that. What more awful thing can humans do to one another? It is like finding someone sick with thirst and drinking water in front of them.

It was painful for Steve and me because any blessing that you try to hoard for yourself begins to sour. We ruin the goodness of friendship when we refuse to use it to bless others, and my memory of being consumed with judgmental pride crowds out my memories of much else in that season. Like peering into stagnant water, my recollection of who I became in that time makes me recoil.

How to Embrace Healthy Limits
While Avoiding Exclusion

Before we go on, we need to pause for a moment and talk about an important distinction. There is a crucial difference between unhealthy exclusion and healthy limits.

You certainly cannot be friends with everyone. You also cannot be friends with just anyone. Because you are not God. You are not everyone's savior. You have natural limits. Limits on your time, limits on your personality, and limits on your capacity to invite others in.

There is a natural limitation to a circle of friendship that is not only perfectly fine but actually really good. The "You too!?" moment inherently means we are at least in some sense turning away from everyone else and turning toward a friend. There is absolutely nothing wrong with this.

In fact, I will defend a kind of exclusion for the sake of deepening relationship in a moment. If you try to be friends with everyone, you will be friends with no one. As Lewis puts it, "To say 'These are my friends' implies 'Those are not.' . . . Friendship must exclude."[2]

But it doesn't take a philosophy degree to split hairs and realize that there is a difference between focusing on a few

IF YOU TRY TO BE FRIENDS WITH EVERYONE, YOU WILL BE FRIENDS WITH NO ONE.

---

2. C. S. Lewis, *The Four Loves* (San Francisco: HarperOne, 2017), 76, 110.

friendships in order to develop deep relationships and actively trying to keep others out of them. One is running toward people, the other away.

The former I call healthy limits, the latter I call exclusion. Put simply: Don't run away from people. Run toward friendship.

When you shake hands with someone, you are, by definition, not shaking hands with everyone else at the same time. But that is far different from seeing another person with their hand outstretched and refusing to shake it. That act of denial is what I mean by exclusion.

The difficulty is that friendships are, of course, more complicated than shaking hands. There is a lot more room for misunderstanding. Sometimes you will hear people complain that so-and-so is being "exclusive" when so-and-so is simply acting out the reality of friendship. For example, going away on a cabin weekend with some friends by nature means you're not doing it with everyone. Having a weekly hangout to catch up with some friends obviously means you're not doing it with everyone. Telling your secrets to close friends is special because you don't do it with just anyone. These are all healthy limits, not exclusion, though you should not be surprised if someone, standing on the outside, calls it such.

My advice is to be gentle with such critics in your heart. They almost certainly speak out of pain—they long for rich friendship just like you do. Sometimes they speak out of fear that they won't find the same or out of jealousy that building friendships is working for you and not for them. Can we not sympathize!? They may be wrong in mistaking healthy limits for exclusion, but why argue when we could do something much more beautiful: invite them in.

If they decline, then move on and keep running toward friendship. But do not let the fear of seeming exclusive prevent you from the work and gifts of friendship, which by nature have some limits.

None of this is easy. Knowing the difference between doing the work of deepening friendships and doing the harm of exclusion takes wisdom and maturity.

It is an art, not a science.

Open Circles

We may experience a natural jealousy when we see the fruit of real friendships that we do not have. We may feel this ourselves, or we may see others feel it.

The obvious answer is the easy one: invite them in! But it is often not so simple.

One thing I deeply appreciate about my friends is that I see all kinds of open, interlocking circles. Yes, there is a group of us who call one another the Cast, but we also all have deep covenant friendships with people the others don't know. If someone were smart enough to map it all, the picture would probably look like a bunch of interlocking key rings dropped in a pile. A mess of circles stuck together—for better or worse.

This is certainly not easy. It always takes work to add someone new. But healthy friendships do not fear the work. We know that we were blessed in order to bless. I love that if I bring a new friend to a fire pit with my friends, that person will be talked to, asked a lot of questions, welcomed, given a good seat, and invited back. That, to me, is one of the healthiest signs of real friendship.

As David Benner writes, "There should be no place for exclusiveness in friendship. In fact, under normal circumstances, circles of friendship expand as other 'kindred souls' are discovered, each addition to the circle enhancing, not diluting, the value of the network of relationships. Each person in the circle of friendship brings out particular aspects of the personality of each of the others. Each can thus be welcomed rather than warded off as a threat."[3]

IT ALWAYS TAKES WORK TO ADD SOMEONE NEW. BUT HEALTHY FRIENDSHIPS DO NOT FEAR THE WORK. WE KNOW THAT WE WERE BLESSED IN ORDER TO BLESS.

I believe that is wonderful. It is how we can be the body of Christ. We build relationships that are strong enough to invite others in.

The table on the next page suggests some simple ways you might consider making a habit of inviting others in. Each of these may seem like common sense. But remember, the simplest things, like greeting someone and saying their name, can be the most powerful forms of relational hospitality.

I write these ideas, but I can also admit that I am fairly bad at them. I make social missteps all the time and also find myself in a phase of life where the demands of my day-to-day leave little room for new relationships. But there is grace. We are not seeking perfection but an ethic of open circles, and these habits help us continue to work at being people who are open to new relationships, even if we go through seasons where that mostly fails.

3. Benner, *Sacred Companions*, 67.

Ideas for Practicing Open Circles

───── OPEN CIRCLES ─────

Think in open circles, whether you're sitting around a fire or a table or in the corner of a room. Consider how you can arrange your bodies physically to suggest a relational truth—others are welcome to come and talk to you.

───── EXTRA CHAIRS ─────

When you host or eat, consider the idea of an extra chair. Whether you plan ahead of time and invite someone new or are simply open to a last-minute guest, the habit of keeping an extra chair signals a readiness for new friends.

───── HABITS OF GREETING ─────

It is impossible to underestimate the power of greeting someone new. These are (ideally) the things that your mom or dad taught you. And if they didn't, learn them now. When you see someone new, look them in the eye, shake their hand, share your name, and ask for theirs. We tend to remember the beginning and the end of gatherings (we'll talk about this more in the chapter on memory), so the kindness of coming to greet someone by name and then saying goodbye to them by name when you leave is one of the simplest and sturdiest foundations for being relationally open.

───── INTRODUCTIONS ─────

If you are hosting, make a point to introduce new people. I learned this from my father. When we have a newcomer to a family meal, my dad will inevitably at some point, usually before we eat, ask for everyone's attention and introduce how our guest came to be here, explain why they should be honored as a guest, and thank them for coming. This may put some people on the spot, but consider how such an introduction creates a moment for everyone to have shared knowledge and expectation—that this guest is honored and welcome not just to the house but to future relationship.

CURATED GATHERINGS

One wonderful habit is to gather people who "should" know one another. In China, we started a club called the Shanghai Feast Society. We would send anonymous invitations to groups of five or six people we thought should be friends and then treat them to a generous dinner and try to spark conversation. This is far on the formal end, but it was an incredible way to catalyze new relationships. More recently, I think of a time when I invited an old best friend to sit around a fire with a new young friend and try to make a connection. Whether formally or casually, consider inviting new people together on purpose.

NAME TAGS

One way we try to signal relational openness in our church community group is by making a habit of wearing name tags. Of course, we generally do not need them. We're the same fifteen to twenty people who show up over and over. But the week when someone new shows up, name tags make it so easy for that new person to feel like it's normal not to know everyone's name.

CARING

Some people may feel they are too far on the edge to accept an invitation to join a hang out or a small group. I have noticed that caring for those people in their times of need can be a wonderful way to open your circle and extend love. Once when we were new to our church, a friend named Lyric spontaneously brought us homemade bread because she heard about something difficult that happened in our lives. I'll never forget how much I felt invited in by that. Whether it's helping someone move or sending meals when someone's sick, acts of care extended from a friend group can be a powerful way to signal invitation without words.

FOLLOW-UP TEXTS

One way you may try to catalyze and foster new relationships is by sending a text to multiple people after a new hangout, introducing the new person's phone number (assuming you think they would *like* this) and sharing the names and numbers of other people they met. Often this is a simple and kind way to follow up and give a newcomer a touch point for the next step in relationship.

But what about when other people don't take you up on the invitation?

We are sinners, after all, and sometimes those we try to invite in do not take up the invitation. They would rather continue to stand on the outside and complain about how they weren't really invited in.

What do we do about those who stand on the outside? Those who refuse to join in and prefer to talk about how they wish they were invited, even though you have invited them time after time after time? First, again, be gentle with such people. Likely they are in pain and fear or they resent something. Second, pray for them. Their aloofness may be a barrier deep in the heart that only Jesus can tear down. You will find in prayer for them that you develop compassion and come to love them more.

Finally, I encourage you to continue seeking friendship with those who are willing to jump into the arena. Do not spend all your energy trying to placate those who choose to criticize from the outside rather than wade into the messy work of real relationships. I think of Roosevelt's famous quote, "It is not the critic who counts. . . . The credit belongs to the man who is actually in the arena, whose face is marred by dust and sweat and blood . . . who spends himself in a worthy cause."[4]

4. In full: "It is not the critic who counts; not the man who points out how the strong man stumbles or where the doer of deeds could have done them better. The credit belongs to the man who is actually in the arena, whose face is marred by dust and sweat and blood; who strives valiantly; who errs, who comes short again and again, because there is no effort without error and shortcoming; but who does actually strive to do the deeds; who knows great enthusiasms, the great devotions; who spends himself in a worthy cause; who at the best knows in the end the triumph of high achievement, and who at the worst, if he fails, at least fails while daring greatly, so that his place shall never be with

To get into the business of friendship is to jump into the arena and, in the words of Roosevelt, to "dare greatly." It is messy work. It is easy to want real friendship. It is much harder to try real friendship.

When you really begin to work at it, expect detractors. When that small group begins to catch a vision, or when that group of guys or girls begins to form into something, when you feel lives beginning to lean toward relationship and form a center of gravity, do not be surprised if someone outside the arena critiques it. Criticizing from the outside is so easy to do you cannot possibly expect anyone not to do it.

IF FRIENDSHIP HAD TO BE PERFECT, NO ONE WOULD EVER TRY IT. MISTAKES ARE NOT A SIGN YOU'RE DOING IT WRONG, THEY ARE A SIGN THAT YOU'RE DOING SOMETHING AT ALL.

They will say that you should have invited _____, or that it was easy for you because _____, or you could have done better in _____, and you don't realize it but from the outside it seems _____.

The fact is, it's probably all true!

In forming friendships, we are of course going to make mistakes, hurt other people, and do it imperfectly. Grace means we can repent and keep trying. But it certainly doesn't mean that we shouldn't try hard things.

If friendship had to be perfect, no one would ever try it.

those cold and timid souls who neither know victory nor defeat." (Theodore Roosevelt, "Citizenship in a Republic" [address at the Sorbonne, Paris, France, April 23, 1910], in the American Presidency Project, accessed April 16, 2023, www.presidency.ucsb.edu /documents/address-the-sorbonne-paris-france-citizenship-republic.)

Mistakes are not a sign you're doing it wrong, they are a sign that you're at least doing something. So keep trying.

Because being in the arena is what counts.

Inclusion as Evangelism

I am a former missionary to China. But even as a corporate lawyer, I am an ambassador of Christ, and I still think of myself as a missionary to law and business.[5] I think of evangelism like studying the Bible: some people will make a profession out of it, but that doesn't mean we aren't all supposed to do it. Evangelism is the natural byproduct of falling in love with Jesus. We talk about the things we love.

Yet I also believe that I have never lived through a more difficult time for talking about our faith. The modern cultural gap between what we say about our faith and what people understand is ever widening. It is hard to find meaningful shared language to talk about love, faith, God, and ethics.

Here, what many may see as a barrier to evangelism, I see as a call to friendship. Because relationship picks up where language ends.

In a world where our neighbors do not understand our language, friendship—not argument—will become the place of evangelism.

Though admittedly it's anecdotal, I have found this to be true. All the Americans I have seen come to faith in the past two

---

5. "We are therefore Christ's ambassadors, as though God were making his appeal through us. We implore you on Christ's behalf: Be reconciled to God" (2 Cor. 5:20).

decades have done so in the context of friendship with believers. This was not true in China. I saw many, many people come to faith as the result of conversations about faith with strangers. This, I believe, is because China is culturally in a very different place than the West. In China, secularism is an argument. It is a set of propositions that are taken as true and that can be disrupted in apologetic conversation. Consequently, at least during the years I was in China, conversation-based evangelism worked to bring people to Jesus. In the West, however, secularism is not an argument, it is a mood. The functional atheism we experience is not something that most of us have ever thought out, it's just the way we all feel. Anyone who knows relationship knows you cannot disrupt a mood with an argument, you must disrupt it with a presence.

Friendship is that presence. It is the way we invite people to draw near and *experience* alongside us what a life of faith looks like.

In a time and place where the current of loneliness sweeps us downriver to inevitable isolation, you can think of covenant friendships as islands in dangerous waters. They are strongholds where we gather and build fires to warm our cold and tired souls. Keeping the open circle of friendship means we are always looking to pluck people out of the water and invite them to come warm themselves by the fire of friendship.

This ethic of hospitality, I believe, is the way forward for modern evangelism in the West. By coming to experience the fire that Christ creates between us, our neighbors will be drawn in. You may not be able to describe the beauty and warmth of friendship with God in modern language, but anyone who stands next to a fire will feel the heat and see the dance of the light.

So put friendship with Christ and others on display. The beauty of inclusion is that we, in some small but real relational way, invite broken people into the spiritual wholeness of friendship.

Without ever speaking, the beauty of inclusion in friendship nonetheless proclaims something incredible: that we are all messed up and broken, and we all struggle with excluding one another, but we can imitate Christ and invite one another in. That is where the good life is.

The Beauty of Three Strands

You do not need to fear exclusion, but you should see the beauty of inclusion.

It took a lot of time for Steve and me to realize our mistake. But unfortunately, more than time, it took pain.

Eventually, in a story that is long, ugly, and too private to be published, Steve and I hurt this new friend. We showed him all the ways he wasn't fit to be in our inner circle. And then, in no small part because of his faithfulness and patience and hunger to pursue friendship anyway, we came to repent.

The way I often put it, which admittedly leaves out all the juicy details, is that this new friend came to see both how broken Steve and I were and how promising the Jesus we worshiped was, and our friend came to know Jesus through our failures. His name is Matt.

I still marvel that the evangelism of our friendship came through our mistakes as much as through anything else. But that is, after all, how God works. Through our sin and in spite of our failures, we came to see that a cord of three strands is better than two. That open circles are stronger than closed ones. And that the natural end of covenant friendships is invitation, not exclusion.

Matt and Steve and I have now counted one another as covenant friends for decades. My son Asher is named Asher Stephen Matthew Earley in honor of them.

But Matt is not only my friend of decades after whom my son is named, he is also a continual reminder to me of the goodness of the open circle of friendship. He is living proof that covenant friendships multiply and thrive when you invite others into them.

CHAPTER 6

Geography

The Art of Rooting and the

Habit of Proximity

In the spring of 2014, I was about to graduate from law school in Washington, DC, but I had lived in Shanghai, China, for longer than I had lived anywhere besides my childhood home.

I was almost thirty. I had a wife, a wonderful son, another on the way, and I was about to have a law degree. But I didn't have a home.

In the previous decade, we hadn't lived in the same house or apartment for more than two years in a row. At the time, that totaled (at least) eight moves in ten years.

I was typical for an American.

It is totally normal to spend your twenties (or longer) living in a slew of apartments and cities and changing jobs like you change clothes. In some ways, this was wonderful. I gained incredible experience over this time, from being an English major at UVA to being a missionary in China to being a law student in DC. But this kind of life also has consequences.

Place and relationship are far more intertwined than we may think. When you don't know where you belong, it is hard to know who you belong to.

Before this time in my life, I had not considered geography and friendship to be necessarily connected. But with a second son on the way and a demanding corporate lawyering job on the horizon, for the first time I had a vision of the places my future life would happen. I would be caring for kids in the morning and evening, and I would be at the office all day. How would deep relationships possibly happen in the hour or two that were left over unless I was physically really close to them?

For the first time, I wondered whether how I wanted to live relationally should guide where I chose to live physically.

Jobs and Geography

One of the reasons I had never thought about this before was because, like the vast majority of Americans, I had assumed that your job should determine where you live. With law school coming to an end, I figured I would move to New York or maybe back to Shanghai because I assumed pursuing a legal career meant I should be wherever the most prestigious law jobs were located. I don't believe this was a foolish thought or even necessarily an "idol"—I felt called to the law, and I meant to pursue this calling with excellence. But I do think there was an imbalance. I thought of my career narrowly and never considered whether I needed good friends to be a good lawyer. From this perspective, a job determines geography and then you see what happens with relationships.[1]

One reason that the modern current pulls us toward loneliness is because most of us live with a similar assumption. Of course, not every single person all of the time lives this way, but

---

1. Many note the relational consequences of being geographically unrooted. It is interesting that there are now increasing amounts of people moving closer to friends and family—instead of closer to work—for stability and happiness. See Nathaniel Hendren, Sonya R. Porter, and Ben Sprung-Keyser, "There's No Place Like (Close to) Home: New Data Tool and Research Show Where People Move as Young Adults," United States Census Bureau, July 25, 2022, www.census.gov/library/stories/2022/07/theres -no-place-like-home.html; and "Why Americans Move," North American Moving Services, accessed January 2023, www.northamerican.com/infographics/where-they -grew-up.

in general, we assume that our work should determine our geography. The primary reason that Americans move long distances is because of jobs.[2] This is not all bad, but it is very new.

Work did not always determine our geography. In fact, our geography used to determine our work. Throughout almost all of human history, our geography and our work were a product of relationship. Family and community were where we inherited our trades and our towns. We lived where we lived and worked where we worked because that was where our people were.

This flip says a lot about our modern search for identity.

Now the question we ask strangers is, "What do you do?" But that's new. It used to be, "Who is your family?" Who you are is now much more a product of your job and work than a product of your relationships and love. I don't want to suggest these were the good old days we all need to get back to. But I do want us to see that we live in a radically different cultural current than the humans who came before us. This view of work has relational consequences.

Unfortunately, this movement of work to the center of our identities has not made us very happy. Not at all.

There is general agreement that work is now a leading indicator of identity in America. Finding a job that makes them happy is more important to many people than getting married or helping others. There is also general agreement that this has made us miserable.[3]

---

2. Riordan Frost, "Who Is Moving and Why? Seven Questions about Residential Mobility," *Housing Perspectives* (blog), Joint Center for Housing Studies of Harvard University, May 4, 2020, www.jchs.harvard.edu/blog/who-is-moving-and-why-seven-questions-about-residential-mobility.
3. "[I]n a . . . Pew Research report on the epidemic of youth anxiety, 95 percent of teens said "having a job or career they enjoy" would be "extremely or

Unsurprisingly, this gospel of work simply doesn't deliver. I firmly believe in the spiritual value of work. We cannot be who God made us to be without it.[4] But the most powerful lies are half-truths, and the modern current of loneliness tells you that satisfaction in work equals satisfaction in life. It does not. It is necessary but not sufficient. Too narrow of a focus on work can cause us to neglect other foundational building block of life— like friendship.

In the opening of this book, I tried to make the case that we can be lonely with God. Everything else in our lives can be going well, but if relationships are not, then we are fundamentally broken. I also tried to make the case that one of the best metaphors for our reconciliation with Jesus is the one Jesus himself uses—friendship. Becoming more like Jesus necessarily means becoming more like a friend.

BECOMING MORE LIKE JESUS NECESSARILY MEANS BECOMING MORE LIKE A FRIEND.

What I have not written yet is that this "theology of friendship," if I can call it that, is something God was developing in my mind and life during my time in law school. And it became a point of friction for me.

It was my drive to find the most prestigious law school

very important" to them as an adult. This ranked higher than any other priority, including "helping other people who are in need" (81 percent) or getting married (47 percent)." (Derek Thompson, "Workism Is Making Americans Miserable," *Atlantic*, February 24, 2019, www.theatlantic.com/ideas/archive/2019/02/religion-workism -making-americans-miserable/583441.)

4. Ron Sider's famous way of saying this is, "People need Jesus, and they need a job." (Ron Sider, interview with Jill Keliher, video, 1:00, shared in Anna Robbins, "Jesus + Jobs = Justice," MacRae Centre for Christian Faith and Culture, Arcadia Divinity College, September 21, 2017, https://macraecentre.ca/2017/09/21/jesus-jobs-justice/.)

available that determined my moving to DC, and I had assumed that finding the most prestigious job would also determine the city we lived in after law school.

But by the end of law school, I felt a strong conviction that I wouldn't be a good lawyer, a good father, a good husband, or even a good disciple if I wasn't also becoming a good friend.

If the place I chose to live would largely determine my relational life, why then shouldn't I take into account the kind of relational person I wanted to be?

Honestly, I never felt the permission to move for friendships. It is so counter to the modern current of loneliness that I felt I needed someone to tell me, "That is not only an appropriate decision to make, that is a good decision to make."

Made for the Space of Relationships

No one ever gave me permission. Usually, no one ever does. But God did give me prayer.

In that season, Lauren and I prayed a lot about whether we should move for a job and let friends follow or move for friends and let a job follow. As we prayed, I continued to sense a shift in myself and what I longed for. (One of the ways you know prayer is working is that it starts to change your desires.)

I felt the Lord turning my mind back to friends over and over. He seemed to be saying, "Yes, I have called you to the law. But you cannot heed my call without covenant friends by your side."

So in that season, Lauren and I made two important decisions.

First, that was the season when we acknowledged the importance of friendships in our lives by deciding to name our second son Asher. We had a lot of good names on the list, but we chose

Asher as a first name because it means "the happiness of God" or "the blessing of God." For his middle names, we chose Stephen Matthew, after the two friends that I told you about. Asher's name reminds me that we find the happiness of God in friendships.

Second, we decided to move to Richmond. Because, well, that was where all of our friends and family lived. This was a big risk. I did find a job there, and a good one. But I also turned down offers at some of the most prestigious law firms in the world. And that worried me. But after much prayer, I felt I had to trust God: if I really was made for people, if friendships were really going to be at the center of life, we needed to treat our geography accordingly.

You Do Not Need to Move!

One of my great goals in life is to see friends become family and family become friends. Nothing has helped that more than rooting geographically. Ten years later, we still live in Richmond. The proximity has allowed weekly family lunches and friend hangouts. It has allowed our kids to see their cousins and call my friends their uncles.

I often think that tying myself to this geography was the best decision our family ever made, because this geography has tied our family to friends.

However, you may be reading this and thinking that all this talk about geography and friendships means you have to pick up and move (or that you made the wrong decision because you moved for a job). Let me assure you—my story should not necessarily be your story.

I suggest you spend your energy rooting where you are rather than thinking about where you are not. Not everyone can or should move, but everyone can and should put down roots. For example, while I happen to live in the same city with covenant friends here in Richmond, as of the time of this writing, I have spent more years living away from them than I have with them. And during those years when I was in China and law school, the practices of phone calls, occasional trips, and cabin weekends held us fast to the gift of friendship even when geography was a barrier. Moreover, I know that all of us have looked for other deep friendships in the places we have lived, even when we knew they were temporary. We will always need a covenant friend or two in the place where we are, which is why we must root where we are.

So no matter where you are, the broader takeaway that everybody in the modern current of loneliness needs to reckon with is that you cannot separate geography and friendship. As you think about growing relationally, you must consider rooting geographically.

This will of course mean different things for different people. There are good reasons for changing homes, cities, and jobs—even God-directed reasons. (Remember, after all, I'm the one who left all my friends and moved to China after college.) But when we get caught up in the cultural current, our decisions to live where we live and go where we go are quick triggered and shallow. That kind of movement guarantees that we will not root.

In pondering this, I suggest two lines of thought. First, consider the ways you are more like a plant than not. Second, consider that you cannot make good decisions about geography all alone.

Like Plants, Relationships Follow Geography

Farmers know that life itself is dependent on land. But we would also do well to realize that more than food comes from land—relationships come from it too.

Unsurprisingly, it takes a farmer to point out how our friendships need soil too. Wendell Berry has been the preeminent author to bring this to the attention of modern Americans. In his writings, Berry makes the argument that we should allow ourselves to be limited and that the good life is not getting rid of all limitations but embracing them.[5]

This is timely wisdom for modern America. We are prone to believe that because we can FaceTime across time zones, we can keep all of our friendships across them too. We are prone to believe that podcasting a sermon is a fine substitute for cramming bodies into pews. We keep assuming that jobs and upward mobility will make us happy and then relationships will follow, and we wonder why we end up richer and yet lonelier. We are prone to think that because we've been "vulnerable" to our social media followers we don't need to sit in the same room with a friend to confess and weep.

But we are wrong. This denial of geography as a catalyst for friendship is really a denial of who God made us to be. We are not spirits who can become technologically omnipresent. We are bodies that desperately need other bodies within arm's reach.

We Need to Reconsider "Family First"

I was talking to a pastor recently, and he noted how many people in his congregation he sees effectively excuse themselves from

5. See, for example, Wendell Berry, *The Unsettling of America: Culture and Agriculture* (Sierra Club Books, 1977).

geographic community by citing a need to put "family first." Often this means a job move or a house upgrade that—because of commute time or impassable distance—makes keeping up former relationships either impractical or impossible.

There is no doubt that the family unit is our strongest temporal and spiritual priority. The firstfruits of our time and energy and resources can, should, and must be given to our family. However, "family first" should not mean "family only," as if all other relationships are optional. Further, it is important to remember that we may not be the best judges of what is good for our families until we make those decisions in community.

WE CAN'T PROPERLY CARE FOR OUR FAMILIES UNLESS WE'RE ALSO CARING FOR OUR FRIENDSHIPS.

My pastor friend noted how putting "family first" in these decisions was usually employed as a conversation stopper that would be better translated as "Don't interfere with the decision I'm about to make." But we need friends to help us make big decisions.

In fact, we cannot do right by our families if we do not keep close friends in the picture. Family, of course, has a natural priority, but it is not our only concern. We would do well to realize that we can't properly care for our families unless we're also caring for our friendships. If we are made for friendship, then we will be missing something fundamental in our marriages and parenting if we try to do those without friends.

The Habits of Proximity

If we're going to swim against the modern current of loneliness, we will need better habits of geography. What would it be like, then, to live as a countercultural church, reimagining our norms of proximity and space in light of relationships? Here are a few examples of what this might look like in your life:

Choose Neighbors Instead of Houses

When Lauren and I bought our house, we had a list of values for our home, but it wasn't all about kitchen size and budget. Those were items, but on our list of highest values was being within walking distance of friends. It is impossible to underestimate the value of choosing neighbors over houses. Sure, a bigger island is great, but we all become relational islands when our main value when buying a home is the kitchen rather than whether people will even come into our kitchens.

Look for Front Porches (Or Things Like Them)

Front porches are where families meet the world. It is no surprise that in an increasingly individualistic age, we focus on back decks rather than front porches. It's not exactly practical to reverse the trends of architecture, so think of this as a metaphor: Where is the gathering space where your family meets the world and sits to talk? Maybe this means putting a picnic table in your front yard, setting up a basketball hoop on the curb, leaving your back fence open, or tearing down a fence between two yards. How is the geography of your home structured to be open to relationships?

Move for Friends

If you happen to be in a phase of life where you are considering moving, consider reversing the default. That doesn't necessarily mean a different decision, it means a different way of coming to a decision. It should be the default that we live near family and friends—unless a calling (which may be an important job) calls us away. So before you pick up and strike across the country, leaving your friends and family in another state, consider whether this is something the Lord is really calling you to or he actually might be calling you to relationships. And vice versa: if you live in another city and have wondered whether you should move to where that place of family and friends is, consider this your prompting to pray about it.

Make Family out of Friends

I know plenty of friends who live far from their families. This distance becomes especially difficult when you begin to have children. The people I see thriving in these situations are the ones who are working to make "family" out of their friends. Whether this is done by trading babysitting, doing sabbath "family" meals together, vacationing together, or something else, if you don't live near your family, consider how you can make the body of Christ the family support network you need.

Worry More about Friend Zones Than School Zones

I know choosing a school for your children is difficult. I also know that not being able to choose a school because of where you live is even more difficult. I do not minimize concern for a child's education (and more important, formation) when it comes to choosing a school. We have chosen carefully for our children. However, it is far too easy to let school choice be consumed by our fears about who our children will become and then move to where we have no friends. Hold the importance of schooling high, but do not forget about another extraordinarily important factor: your kids seeing you in close friendship with other believers. This has an obvious (and proven)[6] impact on your child's walk with the Lord.

There are ways to fill in the gaps of what a school does or doesn't teach, and every school has gaps, but who can fill in the gap of your children growing up in a home with a lonely mother or father who did not model real, vulnerable relationship? So do not stop thinking about the importance of your children's education. But don't neglect their formation either. They need to see you be a friend.

Live Close to Church If You Can

It is hard to emphasize enough how much our community lives would change if we considered geographic location as an important factor when choosing a church. Church can and should be our relational center of gravity. Like everything else in this list, living close to your church is a friendly suggestion, not a command. I live fifteen minutes from my church and pass some thirteen other churches on the drive there, so I don't check this box. We chose our church because we felt called to the urban and missional impulse that it has. But it is worth considering geography on the list of things you pray about as you think about becoming a member of a church.

Claim Sacred Spaces for Gatherings

My friends once dug a huge hole on an undeveloped construction site, called it "the Pit," and made it the center of gatherings

---

6. Don Everts and the Barna Group found in a study of Christian households that one of the most significant indicators of sticky faith for children is having someone of faith outside the family inside the home on a regular basis. See Don Everts, *The Spiritually Vibrant Home: The Power of Messy Prayers, Loud Tables, and Open Doors* (Downers Grove, IL: InterVarsity Press, 2020).

for a whole winter. Before that it was a rope swing on the James River. Then it became the back porch of a house where a few of them lived, and the list goes on. There was nothing special about any of these spaces until they were made sacred by regular gatherings. Gatherings of friendship can make a place into what one might call "thin space"—where the lines between heaven and earth seem to mingle. This is because friendship is a holy thing, and when we visit friendship on a site over and over, the geography has a way of acting back on us. This is not mystical, necessarily (though I'm open to it). It is a simple reality that we attach memories and associations to spaces and open up differently when we go to those spaces with friends regularly. My suggestion is to develop a space like that. Maybe it's your kitchen counter, your dining table, a backyard fire pit, or a park, but consider how you can cultivate a regular gathering space in your normal life to become a sacred space for friendship.

Tie Yourselves Together

A little over a year ago, about ten other friends and I bought a really cheap thirty acres west of Richmond. It's all woods. Mostly thorns. Half flooded and basically undevelopable. (That's why it was so cheap.)

But we bought it because we wanted a place to tie ourselves, and our children, to land—and thus to one another.

Most of us live in the city or the suburbs around Richmond, but all of us long to teach the art of friendship to our children. This is why we were willing to spend a little bit of money on a tangled mess of thorns and swamp: because we weren't getting just land, we were getting an opportunity to leave a legacy of friendship.

To date, we've cut a couple of trails in the woods, started work on a big tree-fort in a grand beech, cleared a place for a firepit, and gotten out for a few camping trips with the kids. Which is to say that mostly, it's all plans for the future. But the land is already beginning to sing with the memories of friendship. In a decade, we hope the song will be heard for miles and miles and all kinds of new people will come dance to it.

TIE YOURSELF TO GEOGRAPHY. BECAUSE GEOGRAPHY WILL TIE YOU TO FRIENDS.

Friendship and geography are intertwined. So my encouragement is this: for your own sake, and for the sake of your legacy, tie yourself to geography. Because geography will tie you to friends.

CHAPTER 7

Time

The Art of Time and the

Habit of Scheduling

In 1914, a man named Ernest Shackleton and his crew of twenty-seven men loaded up a ship called the *Endurance* and set off for Antarctica. Their goal—wait for it—was to be the first people in history to hike across the continent of Antarctica on foot.

Spoiler alert: they did not make it.

The waters off Antarctica were particularly cold that year (can you believe it?) and the ocean froze over while they were still a couple of miles off the coast. So these men were stuck in a ship that was stuck in ice that was stuck at the bottom of the world.

Keep in mind there was no GPS, and radio was still early technology, so no one knew where they were. Do you want to know how long they were stuck there?

Almost two years!

Two years at the bottom of the world where the sun doesn't even come up during the winter months.

This story is told in a book by the ship's name, *Endurance*,[1] and don't worry, this is not actually a spoiler. It's a generally well-known fact of history that Shackleton and all the crew members survived. The question is how they did it, and to get that answer, you need to read the book.

But the only thing more amazing than the fact that they didn't die is that they didn't mutiny either. They became friends.

---

1. Alfred Lansing, *Endurance: Shackleton's Incredible Voyage* (1986; repr., New York: Carroll and Graff, 1999).

If you read *Endurance*, and you should, you'll read a lot about their rhythms of journaling and reading, of eating meals together and talking. As I read the book, I couldn't help but conclude that these simple communal habits became the dividing line between companionship and mutiny, between consciousness and insanity, and eventually, between life and death.[2]

Their ability to hold to patterns, in a real sense, saved their lives.

These people were British sailors, so it might not be surprising to learn that they understood how to keep a schedule. But it is surprising how much a schedule can be the difference between life and death.

Including the life and death of relationship.

The American Ice

The American environment is not friendly to relationship. This is the reality we live in, and this is the environment we have. The question is will we learn not just to survive but to thrive?

It was the winter of 2020—February to be precise—when I sat on my back porch, bundled up under a gas heater, furiously turning the pages of *Endurance* to figure out how, exactly, these sailors survived. (I think I wanted to feel a kinship by reading the book outside in the cold of winter.) I remember thinking for a long time afterward, *What would I do? How would I make it, if extreme circumstances came my way?*

---

2. For accuracy, it is worth noting that this story is not all glory. While the sailors on the *Endurance* stand as a remarkable tale of survival and a testament to the human spirit, other men involved with the same expedition approaching the continent from the other side did tragically die.

With no small sense of irony, two weeks later in March 2020, the whole world was told to go on lockdown.

Sometimes it is the harshest of conditions that teach you what you must cling to.

In the swirl of the first week of that isolation and fear, my friends and I decided on the most outdoorsy and distanced type of gathering we could imagine—a bonfire in the woods. We wanted to be safe and responsible with our bodies, but we also knew we needed to talk for the health of our souls. In retrospect, we intuited something that would later be demonstrated over and over—isolation is just as dangerous to the soul as sickness is to the body.

That evening, one friend who was especially nervous about the virus stood so far from the fire that we occasionally had to repeat things, almost yelling at him to be heard. I remember he felt guilty that he had even come. But I also remember him, over the course of the night, slowly coming closer and closer to the fire as we talked about how we were doing, what we were worried about, how to weather this season with our families and friends, and more.

FRIENDSHIP IS AS URGENT AS IT IS IMPORTANT. SO IT SHOULD BE SCHEDULED AS A WAY OF PRIORITIZING IT OVER THE OTHER DEMANDS OF LIFE.

By the end of the night, he began to talk about how happy he was he came and how he didn't realize how much he needed this kind of conversation with friends.

I think my friend is like most of us.

It is easy to overlook how vital relationship is, so we don't fight to schedule accordingly. Usually, friendship is the last thing we schedule because it feels so flexible. But we are wrong in doing this. Friendship is as urgent as it is important. So it should be scheduled as a way of prioritizing it over the other demands of life.

Over the course of the pandemic, our friends decided that fires such as this needed to be happening regularly, as a scheduled priority. Eventually, some of us began to call these our "Shackleton circles." Meeting around the fire was a pattern we held to, which helped us survive the harsh conditions of the American ice.

In the same way we huddled around a fire to weather the cold, I see us in a much larger way gathered around the fire of friendship to weather the difficulties of life.

Our Troubled Relationship with Time

Remember, the predicament of modern life is that we are prone to become busier, wealthier people who used to have friends. That is the current that takes us should we do nothing else.

Yet this is not how it has to be. You can fight against the current, but the fight for friendship starts with fighting for time.

A fascinating article was written in 2016 called the "The Busy Person's Lies."[3] In it, a woman describes tracking her time for a year to see where it actually went. She, like everyone else, felt tremendously busy, overwhelmed, and stretched thin. She often wondered, *Where did all the time go?*

So she decided to find out by auditing her time for a year. Which, let's admit, is unusual. But why is it unusual? Many of

3. Laura Vanderkam, "The Busy Person's Lies," *New York Times*, May 13, 2016, www.nytimes.com/2016/05/15/opinion/sunday/the-busy-persons-lies.html.

THE CURRENT OF
MODERN LIFE IS TO
BECOME BUSIER,
WEALTHIER PEOPLE
WHO USED TO HAVE
FRIENDS.

us (I hope most of us!) audit our finances. We look at where our money has gone so we can think about whether we're spending it wisely. This is a good thing. Money is a God-given resource, and we should steward it well.

Yet nobody really audits their time. But shouldn't we? If Jesus cared about how we steward our money,[4] wouldn't he care about how we steward our time? Time is the currency of purpose. The thing we each have the exact same amount of every day, and we all get to spend it. The only question is how.

Shouldn't the answer be as important as, if not more important than, how we spend our money? Why don't we track our time more?

Well, this woman did, and the results were as surprising and revealing as you might think. Much of what she found, as a busy working mom, was evidence of a difficult and crazy life—hours in train stations pumping breast milk, hours up in the night caring for children, hours doing laundry and chores. But she also found, for example, she spent 327 hours reading gossip and fashion magazines. She also spent more than 200 hours exercising.

One of her big takeaways was that she had much more agency to choose her time than she thought—but because of her feeling of tiredness, she didn't make those choices properly.

As it turns out, we tend to chronically overestimate—by quite a lot, actually—how much time we spend being productive. One study found that, on average, people estimating seventy-five-plus-hour workweeks were off by about twenty-five hours.[5] On the flip side, we tend to underestimate the time we waste on unproductive things.

4. Matthew 25:14–30.
5. John P. Robinson et al., "The Overestimated Workweek Revisited," *Monthly*

Our struggling stewardship of time shows us two important things. First, we have much more time than we think. But second, we are not good at using that time well because we are often mentally compromised at the moment of choice.

Enter the saving power of a schedule.

Think of a schedule like a parent. When you don't want to get up on time, a parent comes into the room and says, "It's time for school." They keep you honest and move you to the thing you ought to be doing in the moment. The problem is, after we grow up, we don't have a parent anymore. But we don't necessarily get better at choosing in the moment either. We need habits and rhythms to keep us honest. By scheduling things (like time with friends), we introduce accountability and honesty into an important part of our lives: the currency of our purpose. Time.

Scheduling with Friends as a Trellis That Life Grows On

Many people have heard the famous quip by Annie Dillard: "How we spend our days is, of course, how we spend our lives."[6] But you might not know the rest of that paragraph. She goes on to write that a "schedule defends from chaos and whim. It is a net for catching days. It is a scaffolding on which a worker can stand and labor with both hands at sections of time."[7]

I love this image. I think of the city blocks I pass on the way to my office in downtown Richmond, where buildings are

---

Labor Review (June 2011), 49, www.bls.gov/opub/mlr/2011/06/art3full.pdf, quoted in Vanderkam, "Busy Person's Lies."

6. Annie Dillard, *The Writing Life* (1990; repr., New York: Harper Perennial, 2013), 32.

7. Ibid.

surrounded by scaffolding and workers stand up, laboring at the creation of something new. Our days are more like that than not.

We stand on the scaffold of a schedule, working to create something great in life. I think the reason I cling to this image so much is because it gets to the heart of the purpose of a schedule, which is not to stifle meaning in your life. It is the opposite. A schedule is the way you reclaim this currency of purpose called time. It is the way you grab it and use it well.

Many fear that schedules—especially when it comes to relationships—will make things rote or stifle spontaneity. I used to worry the same. Until I realized that most of us—like the woman who tracked her time pointed out—aren't very good decision makers in the moment. So why leave it to the moment? Why not use your best moments to make a schedule and then let it guide you to good places?

In this sense, a schedule is much more like a trellis. It's the scaffolding on which life grows.[8] Why not build a trellis that grows toward lifelong friendships?

At times Lauren and I have stumbled on this accidentally.

Years ago, I heard about two couples who did "Wednesday Night Wine" together and had done so for years. After hearing this, Lauren and I asked another couple if they wanted to do a monthly evening together. I recall that the request alone was meaningful because it gave rise to us all having a conversation about how we wanted to push farther into our friendships. When you make someone an ongoing part of your schedule, something even bigger happens: you make them an ongoing part of your life.

---

8. For a much more developed argument for this metaphor, see my book *The Common Rule* (pp. 1–17 and 95–110), where I discuss setting up a trellis for life in daily and weekly habits, one of which is the habit of friendship.

In reality there were months we skipped and seasons of off time, and eventually more children interrupted the rhythm altogether, but for a season our monthly evenings together became a scheduled pattern of intertwining our lives.

I see now this is what the Shackleton circles did. The fires provided a weekly center of gravity to pull people out of the dark of isolation and into the warmth of friendship. I have also noticed this happen with friends along the way when we have set up weekly coffees.

WHEN YOU MAKE SOMEONE AN ONGOING PART OF YOUR SCHEDULE, SOMETHING EVEN BIGGER HAPPENS: YOU MAKE THEM AN ONGOING PART OF YOUR LIFE.

Notice that my examples here are in the past tense, and that is fine. Schedules are not rules you must follow for the rest of your life or you are a failure. Not at all. But schedules are scaffolds for a season that provide the structure of relationship. Schedules are rhythms that we can dance to, ways we can move in the right direction.

The table on the next page shows some ways that I have seen schedules give life to all kinds of friendships over the years.

Needless to say, I do not keep all of these schedules right now. It would be overwhelming. These rhythms stop and start, they come in seasons, they get interrupted, and that is all fine. Because *all* of them in their season serve an incredible purpose—to work back against the chaos of normal life that drags us into loneliness. That is the saving power of a schedule.

What is far more overwhelming than thinking about the rhythms of friendship is getting dragged along in the busyness of modern life.

WEEKLY COFFEE

Before I had young children (who, in this phase of life, demand most of my morning time), I had various weekly coffees set up with friends where we checked in, talked about life, shared problems, prayed for each other, and enjoyed the morning air. Setting up a weekly coffee for a season with a friend is a tremendous way to spark a deeper level of friendship.

WEEKLY FIREPIT

This is what my friends defaulted to during the pandemic season, and it went such a long way to sustaining us during a difficult time. Not everyone came every week, of course, but establishing a rhythm and expectation during that time that the guys would meet on Saturday (and giving our wives an opportunity to do the same on Friday) became an anchor of relationship during a time when it was very easy to drift down the current of loneliness.

EVERY-OTHER-WEEK PORCH NIGHT

In difficult seasons of life, anything weekly might be too much. My friends Matt and Steve and I wish we were getting together every week, but the reality is that aiming for every other week is more realistic right now. During the writing of this book, we've sat on my porch every other Tuesday night and done a radical thing: told the truth about our lives.

WEEKLY CHECK-IN CALL

I also have weekly touch points with at least two friends right now in the form of brief calls or emails, where we share how certain things are going. Some of this is accountability. Never underestimate the power of friendship in accountability rhythms. We never change alone, but we often change together.

(continued)

QUARTERLY COCKTAILS

I mentioned earlier that I have friends whom I don't often hang out with but nonetheless consider dear friends and want to see regularly. Remember: regular does not have to mean frequent. For the past two years I've had a quarterly cocktail evening that has allowed me and two other friends to catch up even though we go long seasons without much more. Whether it's a quarterly cocktail, cookout, or coffee—whatever you bond over, set a rhythm for it.

MONTHLY SLEEPOVER

Early in my marriage to Lauren, we realized that hanging out with my sister and her husband (who got married six months before us) was lifegiving because we could all process our young marriages together. In our young twenties and only one city away, we decided that once a month driving the hour to where they lived and sleeping over for an evening was a rhythm we should commit to. Just last month, we got our families together (now a combined eight children between us) for a weekend and reminisced on how those monthly sleepovers were such a lifeline of friendship for us in that time. If you're in a phase where that is an option, then intertwine your lives with others for a season.

SECOND TUESDAY OF EVERY OTHER MONTH GET-TOGETHER

This is a mouthful, I know. And that is the point. Sometimes, something off the wall makes sense. I have a friendship now that is part mentorship and part friendship, and this friend asked if we could find some regular rhythm to spending time together. I knew we couldn't do every month, but every quarter seemed like too little for what we were hoping to accomplish, so for about a year now we've attempted to hang out the second Tuesday of every other month. Despite the strangeness of that schedule, it's amazing what the Lord has done in those meetings over the past year. He has continued to knit together a bond of friendship that gives us both life. No matter how odd the rhythm, expect the Lord to be faithful to honor it.

THURSDAY DINNER

Our family is currently in a yearslong rhythm with our friend Drew, who joins us for family dinner every week. In *Habits of the Household*, I write at length about how opening your home regularly can be a way of practicing a rhythm of hospitality. If you're in a stage with a lot of kids, like we are, consider the simple art of opening the mess of your home regularly as a way to practice friendship as a family. Friendship is messy; your house can be too. It's the rhythm, not the neatness, that matters.

MONDAY LUNCH

I currently meet with a great friend who is about a decade younger than me every Monday at 1:30 p.m. to talk about how he is growing with the Lord. You might call this discipleship. You might call it life coaching of the spiritual variety. That's the wonderful thing about friendship: it has the capacity to be many of these things. He doesn't drink coffee, and I usually bring lunch, but 1:30 p.m. on Mondays is the time we meet up anyway and talk about what the Lord is doing in his life. It's been amazing to see the way the Lord has used that time, and I couldn't be more grateful to get a seat to watch what the Holy Spirit is doing once a week.

Every other Tuesday night when I'm supposed to spend meaningful time with Steve and Matt, I have work that I'm putting off. It might be picking up the kitchen, it might be urgent client work, but there is always something. A schedule helps you get better at saying no to the tyranny of the urgent so you can say yes to what is really important—cultivating a life of friendship.

The Extraordinary Power of Ordinary Schedules

When I think back to the Shackleton story, what should have happened to the *Endurance* sailors is predictable. Like the crew members of other failed explorations, they should have starved, gone insane, and died alone in the dark. But what did happen is incredible. In the middle of a ship, in the middle of a polar night, in the middle of the ice sat men huddled around a paraffin lantern, telling jokes, writing in journals, and becoming friends.

Out of the most ordinary rhythms, one of the most extraordinary stories of survival and friendship was born.

We live in a climate that is hostile to friendship. But we can fight against the current. Schedule ordinary rhythms of friendship and watch them lead to extraordinary lives.

CHAPTER 8

Communication

The Art of Communication and the
Healthy Habits of Technology

On a regular Wednesday night, my friends and I had a riveting and spirited discussion on the spiritual responsibility of celebrity pastors. There was plenty of disagreement. We also exchanged tips on bow hunting, shared information on what workouts we were doing that week, complained about infants who woke us up in the night, and discussed prayer and fasting for a friend facing a major career decision. Oh—and my little sister got engaged. So we talked a lot about that too.

It was quite a conversation for an average Wednesday, and it was all thanks to the remarkable gift of text chains.

But there is more. In the past year we've also had several group fights about discussions that many perceived as insulting and derogatory. We have lost untold hours to swiping our phones when we should have been spending time with kids. And we have, with no sense of irony, established text chains and group chats where we've shared our phone usage stats to try to get better at this. We've gotten mad at one another for not reading our messages right or not responding quickly enough. We've also accidentally left people off text invites for parties and then realized our mistake.

That was all thanks to the remarkable curse of text chains.

I mean both with all my heart. Technology is one of the greatest gifts and one of the greatest curses of our time. Every day I see technology used well to deepen real friendships. Every day I also see the misuse of technology whisking people away into "connected isolation," appearing to be surrounded by people and yet functionally alone and isolated.

Technology will either push us farther into friendship or drive us into dangerous loneliness. There really is no neutral, no in-between. Which means that we have a great burden and responsibility when it comes to learning how to redeem technology for relational purposes.

Social Media Snacking

One of the greatest dangers technology has brought to the modern world is fake food.

Since the advent of fast and processed foods in America, for example, public health has become crippled with the problems of preventable diabetes and heart conditions. It is quite possible that eating fast and processed foods may now kill more people than smoking.[1]

Why? Because these foods give us the feeling of being full while leaving our bodies unnourished.

We have the same problem when it comes to relationships. Technology can give us the sensation of being known when, actually, we are completely isolated.

This happens in a myriad of ways. A comment or a like on social media can give you the feeling that you've been social while leaving your soul-deep need for friendship unnourished. Leaving a post or a video can give you the sensation of vulnerability without anyone being there to love you back. Amassing followers

---

1. Joel Fuhrman, "The Hidden Dangers of Fast and Processed Food," *American Journal of Lifestyle Medicine* 12, no. 5 (April 2018): https://doi.org/10.1177/1559827618766483.

creates the real sense of being surrounded by friends, and yet none of them are committed.

The promise of social media is to be fully seen and fully liked. But the promise of covenant friendship is to be fully known and fully loved. The two are very different.

But social media is not the only culprit here. Texting an apology may paper over something that happens, but where is the hug or the tears or the holding of hands to signal forgiveness? Sending a picture of your day is a great update but is no substitute for a shoulder beside you. The list goes on.

When we spend our relational time snacking on technology, we will die from the preventable disease of loneliness.[2]

God Saw That Technology Was Good

To understand how dangerous technology can be, we have to understand how good it can be too. This is very important. Why?

First, because technology can and should support our friendships. A good snack can be a bridge to the next meal or just a delightful indulgence. Both are fine so long as the meals stay healthy.

---

2. For the snacking analogy, I am indebted to a conversation with Clayton and Josh during a trip to visit Christ Community outside Chicago, where we ate a fine meal and Josh sparked conversation about how relationships, not social media, are the real meal.

Second, technology is ubiquitous and is not going away. Our primary job is not to resist technology but to use it in relationally healthy ways. Just like with eating, the goal is not to say no to snacks but to cultivate a love for healthy food.

So consider with me a moment how good technology can be.

God is a maker, and remember that when he made things, he called them good. He also made us to be makers, so it is good that we, like God, invent things—including technology.

In Genesis, God builds materials for us to discover and use in the garden. "The gold of that land is good; aromatic resin and onyx are also there."[3] So the idea that humans would pick apart, study, rearrange, and use the world not only is contemplated in the Genesis narrative but also is part of God's grand purpose for us.

Think of it like this: When we make communications technology like social media and smartphones, we're not advancing some evil future—as if the past is more righteous simply by being past. We're doing what God made us to do. We're creating. And that's a good impulse.

But unlike God the maker, we are fallen humans. So the act of making in and of itself isn't enough to call what we make good; we also have to examine our creations' purpose. Everything we make, no matter how simple, has a purpose. The fancy word for this is *telos*, the Greek word for "end." Technology wants us to do something with it. It wants us to use it to some end.

This is where technology can become so devastating. The purpose of some technologies is really—like sugary foods—to make money by keeping us snacking. This is sinister and

---

3. Genesis 2:12.

dangerous. We need to get better at recognizing these technologies and resisting them.

But other technologies are designed to allow humans to communicate and relate, and that is an end that God would absolutely call good because it contributes to human flourishing. We should learn to use these technologies in proper ways, even while we carefully ensure they do not become the primary ways we relate.

This is as practical as it is theological. It means we must look at technologies and ask, "Can this be used for relational flourishing?" Most times, I suggest, the answer will be yes.

But we're not quite done. *How* we use technology is equally important.

Use Technology Only for What It Was Made For

I tell my kids something my dad told me: use things only for what they were made for. Otherwise you will break something or someone. It's a tried-and-true piece of fatherly wisdom. Use a computer to hammer a nail, and you will break something valuable. Use a screwdriver as a spoon and you will hurt yourself.

The more complex and powerful the technology, the higher the stakes get. Cars, computers, and prescription medications, for example, are some of the most wonderful and most dangerous technologies you can imagine. Because really good technologies can cause really serious harm if you do not use them properly.

In our modern moment, nowhere is this truer than in communications technology.

The internet and smartphones are fantastic for connections, communication, and knowledge. But connections are not friends, communication is not intimacy, and knowledge is not wisdom. Use a social network for intimacy and you will invite great harm. Use a chat room for wisdom and you are guaranteed foolishness. Use connections for friendship and you are destined for loneliness.

THE INTERNET AND SMARTPHONES ARE FANTASTIC FOR CONNECTIONS, COMMUNICATION, AND KNOWLEDGE. BUT CONNECTIONS ARE NOT FRIENDS, COMMUNICATION IS NOT INTIMACY, AND KNOWLEDGE IS NOT WISDOM.

For most people, the question will be how (not whether) we use technology in relationships. We then must ask, How are these technologies reshaping our friendships, and is that good?

Notice again here that the question is not whether technology is reshaping our relationships; the question is how.

To ignore this question is to float down the current, and there is no doubt the technological current leads to some of the most despairing loneliness the world has ever seen.

Do Not Fear

The stakes of technology use are very high today. But we should not be afraid. While the technologies are new, we are not up against an enemy we've never seen before.

Smartphones are recent, but loneliness and friendship are ancient. Technology has reshaped the world many times over. From the Tower of Babel to the Bronze Age to the printing press to the Industrial Revolution to now, how we use technology in our relationship with God and others has been a constant theme of human history.[4] That said, we are in an absolute time warp of change. This is hard to overemphasize. Bronze and iron reshaped the world over millennia. The printing press rearranged the world over the course of centuries. Television in decades. Social media in only years. Who knows what is next? But this should be a call for humility and wisdom, not fear and anxiety.

Instead of being anxious about what technology might do to our kids, we should be humble about what it is doing to us. Instead of focusing on the fear of what it's doing to other people, we should focus on how we can wisely use it to love other people.

So let us exchange anxiety and fear for sobriety and wisdom and, above all, for love.

I propose a simple paradigm for evaluating relational technology: view all nonphysical interactions as a kind of snack, not the main course of relationship. This is as true for Facebook as it is for virtual church attendance. Use it sometimes in some ways, and it can be a healthy bridge to get you to your next relational meal. But if you use it to replace the nourishment of friendship and community, you will begin to die of loneliness.

We were made for people. We should throw off all uses of technology that distract us from being fully known and fully loved by friends and embrace all uses that help with that.

How do we do that?

---

4. I've benefitted immensely recently from a long-form podcast by Paul Cooper called the *Fall of Civilizations*, which looks at ancient civilizations and how technologies (among other things) shaped their rise and fall.

Here are some ways my friends and I try to put technology in its proper place[5] in our relationships:

Text Chains or Social Media Chats

As the story about the Wednesday night text chain illustrated, text chains or social media chats are wonderful ways to stay connected to and updated on friends and family. The challenge here is to find limits that help you use these tools for what they are meant for—short connections that help you be known—and not as substitutes for in-person conversations where you can become fully known. Further, they are great when they are tailored toward the limited number of friends you have rather than the unlimited number of companions (or followers) you might have. Followers are simply not friends.

I love using text chains or messaging apps for announcements, daily updates, pictures, accountability, planning, and much more. But notice that these things are not the deep fodder of relationship. My friends and I have impassioned spiritual and political discussions (and arguments) on text threads, but we also recognize there is a limit.

First, there is a limit to the love you can show. When we first began to actively use messaging to keep up with one another, we found that it was way easier to misunderstand one another and be hurt by sarcasm. It was way harder to experience real encouragement. This is a serious limitation. You may be able to text

---

5. While not specific to friendship, this phrasing and the idea of the "proper place" for technology are very helpfully detailed in Andy Crouch's *The Tech-Wise Family: Everyday Steps for Putting Technology in Its Proper Place* (Grand Rapids: Baker Books, 2017).

some meaningful updates, but to be fully loved in return almost always requires bodily presence.

For example, we once had an argument over something in the news that got so heated that we decided to all sit down and discuss. We found within thirty minutes that we were all 95 percent in agreement, and the remaining 5 percent of disagreement did not seem nearly as important as it had over text message. Ever since we've had a signal—we send a campfire GIF if a discussion is getting too heated. The fire GIF signals that we've reached the end of our ability to meaningfully discuss or argue about a topic on text message, and we need to meet in person (preferably around a backyard fire).

There is a real limit to what we can communicate without tone and facial expression. In the past year, I've had two serious sit-downs with people to talk about misunderstandings that happened via text. After a few of these conversations, I resolved never to use sarcasm in a text because it just hasn't helped any of my relationships. I've also committed to never send anything angry in a text because those discussions need to be in person. My friends know this, by the way, and they are the first to remind me of my "solemn vow" (as one friend calls it) if I send a sarcastic or snippy text.

I don't think this means we should stop messaging so much. I just think it means we should continue sitting down more and recognizing that vital, but intangible, aspects of our relationships require our being together.

Another thing we can't do via text is pray for one another. We can talk about prayer, and that is great. We have so many prayer requests and answered prayers that pass through text. But that does not substitute for when I pause to actually pray, or when I sit down with a friend and pray for them or with them about what they have shared.

I suspect everyone's limits will be a bit different, but I'd encourage you to embrace habits of texting that keep you close to friends while recognizing the limits and committing to the regular and frequent face-to-face meetings that are required for real disagreements, real vulnerability, real solutions to problems, and real prayer together.

The snack cannot replace the meal.

Social Media Platforms

You cannot, and should not, be carrying out real relationship on social media. That may sound odd after I just endorsed texting or messaging as a meaningful way to stay connected. Here is why. You pay for text messaging. It's a phone plan or an internet plan. As a result, texts have little incentive to make any more money off you. It's a fairly simple transaction.

Social media has a very different goal (*telos*) for you. You generally don't pay for it, so social media needs to find a way to make money off you. Which means that it will use all its tools (and the highly educated and wildly paid programmers on the other side of the screen have lots of tools) to funnel you into different interactions.

Friendship may be an essential resource. But friendship is not a commodity. People cannot make money off it. Which means that social media is not incentivized in any meaningful way to push you into friendship. You may think I'm cynical—but I encourage you to be wise and live with open eyes. Social media programmers are usually smarter than you, and you would do well to be skeptical.

It is true that you can message people, update friends, post pictures of your life—and I do all of that. You can follow me on Twitter and Instagram and call me a hypocrite for criticizing social media. But I am very comfortable using it for limited purposes. And I suggest you set careful limits too.

Use it for what it is—a marketing tool that allows you to share your ideas with the rest of the world. It's not meant to be a place for true vulnerability, unfiltered relational communication, or real connection in any sense.

I also strongly urge you not to waste your vulnerability on social media. For example, I suggest that it is dangerous to post a picture of yourself crying and share your woes to the public and let that scratch your itch to be known even though you come away alone and thus unloved. Instead, you should embrace the real relational intimacy of in-person friendship where you can't control the way you look when you cry, you can't filter the messy house out of your background, you can't reword things one million times before saying them, and you can't edit them once said.

THAT UNVARNISHED DANGER IS WHAT MAKES FRIENDSHIPS SO MESSY AND SO INCREDIBLE. ONLY IN THE IN-PERSON WORLD OF RISK DO WE HAVE THE CAPACITY FOR REAL VULNERABILITY AND REAL LOVE.

That unvarnished danger is what makes friendships so messy and so incredible.[6] Only in the in-person world of risk do we have the capacity for real vulnerability and real love.

6. Sherry Turkle, in her book *Reclaiming Conversation: The Power of Talk in a Digital Age* (New York: Penguin Books, 2015), 143, writes of students she has interviewed who

Video, Calls, and Group Calls

Notice that the more instant a medium becomes, the more it is able to handle true relationships. There is a reason for this. The more real time and the more intangibles we can pick up on, the better the relationship is. We are embodied people, and when we mediate ourselves through text mediums or social media, we lose a lot. I think calls and video chats are one place where more is preserved than lost, and we can use them accordingly.

I have important weekly phone calls that serve as great accountability mediums. I have times where I can't make a regular hangout because of work or parenting obligations, but I happily default to a call instead to save time but preserve relationship. I have times where one friend can't make a porch sit, but we set up a chair and FaceTime him in to at least approximate some of the hangout we intended to have. I have even had parties that I have video called into because I was traveling and sitting in a lonely hotel while all my friends were getting together—and it was worth it to have the phone passed around.

All of this is lovely and goes a long way to encourage friendship across distance.

However, when you lose physicality, you lose much more than you think. When you see a friend and give them a hug, a high five, or a fist bump, or you throw an arm around their shoulder, so much more is happening to you than you may realize. You are being altered by the loving physical presence of another. You need this. We need this physicality. Try parenting over FaceTime and you will immediately realize how much is

claim they prefer online conversation because "unrehearsed 'real-time' conversation is something that makes you 'unnecessarily' vulnerable." But vulnerability is the point of embodied relationships.

lost when you cannot be physically present with your children. But children are not the only ones whose sense of love is deeply informed by physicality. This is true for all of us.

Phone and video calls are a poor substitute for the best of our lives when proximity to someone's body changes how we interact with them. When I am with my close friends, sharing something important or confessing something vulnerable, I am watching their faces for winces of "I wish you hadn't said that," or nods of "I feel and understand." So much is happening when we think nothing is happening, and I suggest that you need your friends' bodies more than you think.

It is very possible that by the time you read this, all of these technologies will seem quite dated. That is fine, because technologies change. But here is what does not change: the miracle of human presence. We are made for people, and we will always need the embodied presence of human beings to do that central thing God made us to do: love him and love others. So use technologies for what they are good for, but do not substitute them for the thing you need most: to be vulnerable and loved in the presence of a friend.

Gather around the Fire

As I mentioned at the beginning of this chapter, my friends and I carried out a riveting debate via text one Wednesday night. I suspect the next time I open my phone I will find untold numbers of my friends' hilarious GIFs, menial updates, incredible prayer requests, and more.

But one thing I know for sure is that when I open it, I will see plans for the fire one of us is hosting this weekend. All of the families in town are coming. Everyone's bringing kids. We'll have a fire late into the evening, long after the children are sent home and put down for bed. And that, far more than any other message I get on social media today, far more than any other work email, far more than any other Zoom call, is going to change my life.

One of the oldest technologies is fire. When it comes to friendship, I suggest sticking to that one. People have been gathering by fireplaces, firepits, and all the other things like it for millennia.[7]

When we gather fireside, we have the sense that something third is there. Something warm, something to gaze at, something to gather around. We sense it because it is true. Something, or rather someone, else is there. It's the Holy Spirit, who comes in fire and promises he is present when any two friends of Jesus are gathered.

There is something real—however intangible—to embracing that truth in a bodily manner. Technology will change your friendships, for better and worse. So choose it very carefully, and don't make meals out of snacks. While some technology is great, I humbly suggest you stick mostly to the technology of fire.

---

7. For more background on why fire is so relationally significant and how to bring it into friendships, see the chapter entitled "Close" in Jennie Allen's excellent book *Find Your People: Building Deep Community in a Lonely World* (Colorado Springs: Waterbrook, 2022).

CHAPTER 9

Memory

The Art of Memory and the

Habit of Living on Purpose

My sons were as excited as I was to help pack the car, even though they weren't going anywhere.

We loaded up a tent and a sleeping bag, a stainless-steel French press, and a bottle of good whiskey into their uncle Matt's '94 Toyota Land Cruiser.

Steve and Matt and I headed out on a twenty-four-hour getaway. We four-wheeled up a mud trail in the Blue Ridge to the top of a mountain where you can get a view of the valley with no one else around. We set up a simple camp, put chairs around the fire, made rib eye steaks, and talked the night away. There was no grand hike the next morning. There was no special activity. I made pancakes (as one does when camping), we had a strong cup of coffee to power through the unidentified whooping bird that robbed us of our sleep from one until two in the morning, we stopped briefly at a mountain lookout on the way home to say a prayer together, and then we got back to our families by early afternoon the next day.

This is not a time of life when we can all just get away. As with friendship itself, we have to fight for these times.

A couple of months ago some of our wives did their version of the same (though they got two nights at an Airbnb, which was considerably more comfortable than our campsite!) while the guys took all the kids for the weekend. This happens in all kinds of varieties. A weekend for a bachelor party or a wedding. A camping trip. A guys' retreat or a girls' retreat.

These rhythms may be infrequent, but therein lies their power. Each one carries a unique opportunity to rejuvenate and revive friendships in a way that an evening in town does not.

Why? Because our brains latch onto moments. Our souls crave memories. Much of what we share when we call ourselves friends are shared memories of moments that stand out from the norm of life and change the way we see ourselves and our friends.

Our memories with friends form a deeply spiritual part of who we are.[1] We should be looking for such opportunities to seek meaningful conversations and to make rich memories that become a shared spiritual heritage.

The Shaping Power of Extraordinary Moments

A famous quote often attributed to Ralph Waldo Emerson reads, "I cannot remember the books I've read any more than the meals I have eaten; even so, they have made me." I love that thought. I can't recall most dinners, I forget too many books, and I don't remember 90 percent of the sermons I've heard; and yet all have sustained my body and soul in ways I cannot even begin to fathom. I might not be able to recall the vast majority of my conversations with friends, but I know they have sustained my soul through the years.

What really shapes us is the small stuff. Habits form most of our lives. Yet there are a couple of sermons that caused tectonic

1. For a compelling exploration of the role of memories in spiritual formation, see Casey Tygrett, *As I Recall: Discovering the Place of Memories in our Spiritual Life* (Downers Grove, IL: InterVarsity Press, 2019). Tygrett says, "We lose our selves when we lose our memories, and without our memories, growth and formation simply wander into oblivion" (11).

shifts in the way I think. There are a couple of weekends that pushed my friendships to another level.

Memorable moments matter. Habits and ordinary moments may be the foundation of life, but they are not all there is to life. There is another reality, and that is the power of extraordinary moments that totally reshape us.

While psychologists have done a lot to show that our lives are shaped by habit,[2] they have also shown that what we remember about our lives is different. For example, studies show that as we reflect back on experiences, we are more concerned with the peaks or the ends of experiences, as opposed to the bulk of them that we actually spent our time on.[3] This is why, for example, you could have a great day with your children, but then when it ends in a tantrum and meltdown, you reflect on the whole day poorly—even though that was only a small part. Likewise, it's why we value a getaway with friends as a memorable, peak moment that stands out from the life of friendship that sustains us week to week. That daily sustenance is more important, but also more forgettable.

Those peaks shouldn't be ignored. They form our memory,

I MIGHT NOT BE ABLE TO RECALL THE VAST MAJORITY OF MY CONVERSATIONS WITH FRIENDS, BUT I KNOW THEY HAVE SUSTAINED MY SOUL THROUGH THE YEARS.

---

2. See, for example, two of the best summaries on this: Charles Duhigg, *The Power of Habit: Why We Do What We Do in Life and Business* (London: Random House, 2013); and James Clear, *Atomic Habits: An Easy and Proven Way to Build Good Habits and Break Bad Ones* (New York: Avery, 2018).

3. Daniel Kahneman, *Thinking, Fast and Slow* (New York: Farrar, Straus and Giroux, 2011), 380–88.

which also means they form our perceptions of our relationships. They form who we are and who we believe our friends are. We shouldn't ignore that formation just because it's not the most important. On the contrary, we should embrace it. Put otherwise: "Defining moments shape our lives, but we don't have to wait for them to happen. We can be the authors of them."[4]

Jesus at the Campfire

You can create rich experiences with friends in lots of ways, but (as you have surely picked up on throughout this book) I'm partial to campfires and cooking. I think I have good reason for it.

One of my favorite chapters in the Bible is John 21. I've always been intrigued by John—he feels like the "writer's writer" of the Gospels. He extends the stories, adds a literary flourish, and leans into metaphors. For that reason, John's retelling of the last days of Jesus with his disciples is absolutely captivating.

Remember where Jesus and his disciples are in their life together at this point. Jesus has died and risen. He has appeared to them but not been clear on what's next. I sense they feel like kids in their last morning at summer camp—they realize this has been amazing and are now facing returning to normal life. They don't really know what's next.

It's also important to remember they are a group that has experienced serious collective trauma and shock. They all watched Jesus get captured and killed days ago. And yet they have also experienced collective awe—the risen Lord has appeared to them. It has been a big couple of days to say the least. They are all

---

4. Chip Heath and Dan Heath, *The Power of Moments: Why Certain Experiences Have Extraordinary Impact* (New York: Simon and Schuster, 2017), 5.

trying to figure out what this means. Peter, in particular, is still reeling. He denied his beloved friend *three* times amid all that. He abandoned him in his moment of crisis. He is reeling with shame.

In short, they are a lot like us on a normal day. We're confused about what's next, half numbed by the trauma of life, and clouded by our shame.

It is in this difficult time that Jesus catches them and changes them with the power of an extraordinary moment.

First, note that when the disciples' boat is far out in the water and they have no idea who is onshore yelling to them, Jesus calls out, telling them to throw their nets to the other side. Sound familiar?

This is, of course, how Jesus originally encountered Peter,[5] after a night of fruitless fishing, telling him to cast his nets out into deep water. In Luke, when this first happens to Peter, he falls at Jesus' knees for the first time. Here again, at the end of their years together, Peter realizes that this is Jesus standing on the shore, and he leaps into the water (perhaps in his underwear!)[6] and runs to him.

Jesus has kicked off a moment, triggering important parts of Peter's memory. But he is not done yet.

Next, as the rest of the disciples get to shore, he cooks them fish over a charcoal fire. Seems like an eccentric detail to include, right? Jesus the campfire cook? But let us pause for a moment and realize that the Lord of the universe, in one of his most important moments with some of the most important

---

5. Luke 5:1–11.
6. "Then the disciple whom Jesus loved said to Peter, 'It is the Lord!' As soon as Simon Peter heard him say, 'It is the Lord,' he wrapped his outer garment around him (for he had taken it off) and jumped into the water" (John 21:7).

people in the world, simply chooses to cook for them. To serve them. As if simply eating together just might lead to one of the most important things in the world—fellowship.

During that fellowship, they do something mundane together. Count fish. You read that right. In their final moments with the risen Lord and Savior Jesus Christ, Jesus deems it worthy for the disciples to tend to their day's work and count their haul. I imagine them dropping the fish from one pile to the other while they stand around the way men do, mumbling about the process.[7] It is fascinating that even in this extraordinary moment, Jesus is attentive to their ordinary concerns.

Next, remember that odd detail amid this cooking and counting? The charcoal? We are told specifically that Jesus was cooking over a "charcoal" fire, which happens to be the second of two times this word is used by John (a writer who chooses every word on purpose). The first time was just a few days back, when Peter stood around a charcoal fire denying Christ three times.

Finally, surely connected to this denial of Peter, Jesus strikes

---

7. Counting the fish may seem like a tangent, but it's worth exploring. Here is one of the most delightful passages ever written on it: "This is, it seems to me, one of the most remarkable statistics ever computed. Consider the circumstances: this is *after* the Crucifixion and the Resurrection; Jesus is standing on the beach newly risen from the dead, and it is only the third time the disciples have seen him since the nightmare of Calvary. And yet we learn that in the net there were 'great fishes' numbering precisely 'an hundred and fifty three.' How was this digit discovered? Mustn't it have happened thus: upon hauling the net to shore, the disciples squatted down by that immense, writhing fish pile and started tossing them into a second pile, painstakingly counting 'one, two, three, four, five, six, seven . . .' all the way up to an hundred and fifty and three, while the newly risen Lord of Creation, the Sustainer of all their beings, He who died for them and for Whom they would gladly die, stood waiting, ignored, till the heap of fish was quantified. Such is the fisherman's compulsion toward rudimentary mathematics! . . . [Or,] another possibility occurs to me: perhaps they paid the fish no heed. Perhaps they stood in a circle adoring their Lord while He, the All-Curious Son of His All-Knowing Dad, counted them all Himself!" (David James Duncan, *The River Why* [San Francisco: Sierra Club Books, 1983; repr., New York: Back Bay Books, 2016], 20, 22.)

up an incredible conversation with him that everyone is standing around to watch: Jesus asks Peter if he loves him. Three times!

Pause for a moment to consider the awkwardness. The public nature of it. The repetition. Peter says yes each time, but Jesus seems not to accept his answer, repeating the question until Peter, exasperated, says, "Yes! You know I love you."

What's going on in this story?

Memory.

Jesus is acting out an extraordinary placement and curation of defining memories into the lives of the friends he loves. In some ways he reinforces wonderful old memories, and in other ways he tries to replace bad and shameful memories with better ones.

Jesus is redeeming the memories of his friends by creating new memories. He's weaving a new fabric of relational shalom in their minds. By using taste and smell and events they've experienced before, he's harking back to times they had together; he's rehashing things they've said—all for a reason.

He's trying to let his unending grace sink down to the bone level of their memory.

He is doing this so his disciples feel, as much as they know, that he is the lover of their souls.[8]

The Master of Experience

What can we take from Jesus' use of extraordinary moments to shape the people he loves by a memory? Really, there is no end.

---

8. For these insights I'm indebted to Curt Thompson's *The Anatomy of the Soul: Surprising Connections between Neuroscience and Spiritual Practices That Can Transform Your Life and Relationships* (Downers Grove, IL: InterVarsity Press, 2010), 226–28.

Jesus, of course, is the ultimate friend. And here we would do well to imitate him as the master of friendship.

Jesus is using experiences that call to mind the beginnings of relationships. He is incorporating experiences that honor the ordinary—"How have you been? Catch me up. How many fish have you caught?" He understands that experiences that serve—"Let me feed you"—set people at ease. He goes deeper and pushes into experiences that reverse shame by allowing someone to walk over the memories of the bad and replace them with the good. He leans into experiences where intentional and awkward conversations are had so that "I love you" can be said and remembered when it so often goes unspoken.

We can learn from all of this as we consider how we can intentionally create memories that, on a deep level, remind us as friends that we are known and loved anyway.

In the churn of day-to-day life, it is difficult to hold on to the anchors of relationship. My friends and I often poke fun at our friend Matt, who admits that if we go a few weeks without hanging out, he feels like we have forgotten him and that maybe we were never actually friends.

We laugh, but there's a good point behind Matt's humorous complaint. Friendships need to be protected and, in some senses, resurrected by creating memories to reinforce that we are indeed one another's beloveds. Creating moments outside the ordinary is one of the best ways to care for the ordinary. But that takes living on purpose. And Jesus is the expert of living on purpose.

If you zoom out, this scene begins to look like a curated experience that Jesus was leading his friends through. Jesus is the consummate host. Even on a beachside camp at dawn, Jesus has plotted experiences that will work grace into his friends' memories.

I call this kind of thing "living on purpose." It means trying to shape the ordinary moments with your friends instead of letting life shape you. It doesn't have to be anything grand, it simply means living purposefully into moments of friendships in order to shape your memories of them.

Here are some ways to make living on purpose a norm. I will not be original. Instead, I'll riff off Jesus, the master of memory and relationships, and hope to inspire you to imitate him:

Do Things That Remind You of Your Story

I love that to begin an important moment with his friends, Jesus reminded them of his first encounter with them. There is something unashamedly romantic about it. Like taking your wife back to the first restaurant you ever ate at.

In friendships, I find this can be significant because it reminds us of the ways that God has worked to make us who we are.

This might be meeting up in your college town to have a weekend away, or it may be simply devoting a night to reminiscing with old friends or recounting with a small group what the Lord has done.

A few years ago, some friends and I had a day where we all met up and sat by the river where we used to spend so much time in high school and college. We knew we had only one afternoon together before another friend had to catch a flight and that we wouldn't see one another for months after that. So we took the afternoon off work and sat together on a river rock, remembering the past and talking about the future. Picking that place to sit had no small impact on the nature of the conversation.

Consider how making purposeful space to rehash the

memory of what the Lord has done in your life relationally is a holy and important thing. Looking backward in gratitude can give us vision forward in hope.

Behold Beauty

I don't know that there was anything special to the beach by the sea in Galilee, but I have to imagine a sunrise on that water is about as stunning as a sunrise on any water. It doesn't take a master of relationships to realize that going on a hike, or sitting by the river, or spending a weekend together at the beach or in the mountains does something that staying in our ordinary environments does not.

This could be meeting up with a friend to watch the sunrise and walk. It could be sitting out under the stars with a gigantic bonfire. It might mean kicking up a book club with friends to read a meaningful book together. It might be going to an art gallery and just sitting under the spell of beauty. Recently some friends and I attended a large jazz concert, and taking the moment to get out of ordinary life, listen to spellbinding music, and enjoy time together refreshed us in a way we didn't expect and made for a great evening of relationship to follow.

FRIENDSHIPS ARE NOT ALL MUNDANE ACTIVITY. WE NEED TO BEHOLD THINGS BIGGER THAN US TO BIND US. THERE IS SUCH BINDING POWER IN THE SHARING OF BEAUTY.

Relationships are not all words. Friendships are not all mundane activity. We need to behold things bigger than us to bind us. There is such binding power in the sharing of beauty. It should be sought out on purpose, not ignored.

Cook for One Another

I don't think I'll ever get over the joy and novelty of Jesus the campfire cook. I could dwell on it all day. The Lord of the universe does the simplest things to bless us.

Whether it's a getaway or a regular evening, there is a remarkable power to serving one another through food. In our season of life, blessings (like babies) and tragedies (like sick parents) seem like a monthly occurrence. And I'm amazed at how quickly our friends kick up meal solutions for one another and bring food or send food or just come and sit and cook food for one another.

When we get away and have weekends together or long evenings together, often we spend inordinate amounts of that time cooking together, and that is not lost. The memory of shared enjoyment and service binds our lives together in ways that lead to vulnerability, reliance, and joy.

Last year, my (rather large) extended family rented a sort of compound of cabins to celebrate Christmas in, and my birthday happens to be two days after Christmas. So when we were all together, I asked if we could celebrate my birthday by letting me cook everyone a meal on the campfire outside the cabins. They graciously agreed, and we spent six hours of that afternoon around an open fire where I hung prime rib (you read that right) and slowly roasted it. We laughed and snacked and fussed over the food and kept eating until it got so dark that we had trouble seeing our plates.

Later, my sister told me that my nephew shared at school that the best part of his Christmas vacation was when his uncle cooked a campfire meal for everyone. I love that. Because never mind that I burned my fingers a few times, that the dogs spilled a bunch of things, that a few kids fell apart and needed to be carted off for naps, and that I snapped at other kids who kept getting too close to the fire. There were lots of foibles. But we dropped an anchor in the memory of our friendships as family members.

Food alone is just a big meal, but friendships make a feast. So combine them on purpose. Purposeful feasts have a unique power to shape friendships. The food may be eaten quickly, but the memories will last forever. Feast, then, for the sake of friendship!

Have Catch-up Times

As charmed as I am by Jesus cooking, I'm more charmed by the idea of him counting fish with his disciples. It is a stunning reminder that the Son of God is interested in how your day went, so a friend should be too.

We practice this around the dinner table at night with my boys, asking how school went and insisting on interesting and detailed responses. Why? Because the art of sharing about your day is the early art of learning friendship.

A good friend will want to know how your day went. A good friend also knows how to share how theirs went. This is the basis for much of my friends' texting and accountability hangouts, and yet anyone knows that in the demands of regular life, extended catch-ups of "how things are really going" can be few and far between.

Despite the mundane nature of it, catching up can also be

an important memory. Setting aside an extended time to catch up and listen at length is a meaningful way to create memory and solidify friendship. I have a group of friends that, for four years running now, I have gotten away with for the stated goal of catching up. Last year, we made a list of about ten good questions and everyone had to write out answers ahead of time. (One of the questions our wives had to answer on our behalf.) Then we started a long, long evening catching up by having someone else read each person's answers.[9] Then we asked follow-up questions.

There was nothing special about this except for the remarkable fact that we sat around talking for up to an hour about each person, how their family was, how their heart was, what they were struggling with, what they felt proud of, and more.

Never underestimate the power of being known in the history and details of your life. Never underestimate the significance of a friend knowing how many fish you caught or offering to count them with you.

These conversations are a result of living on purpose. Sometimes rehashing the ordinary moments is an extraordinary act of friendship.

---

9. If it helps, here are our questions:

    1. What has been the biggest change in your life since last year?
    2. What's something you can't stop thinking about or wrestling with?
    3. What's your most exciting vocational opportunity right now? Where does it put you in five years?
    4. What are you missing in your walk with God right now?
    5. What are you proud of right now?
    6. What has made you sad this year?
    7. How would your wife describe how you're doing?
    8. What's one book or podcast everyone needs to pay attention to?
    9. These three questions are for your wife: What's your family's biggest opportunity and biggest challenge? What do we need to push your husband on? What do we need to encourage him on?

Make Time to Process Hard Things

Consider Jesus' deep mercy and kindness in going back to address Peter's defining moment of shame.

We have so much literature and research now about how shame and trauma rearrange our brains and create lasting scars in the memory that can forever change how we act and relate to the world and people. Since the fall, it seems our sins really do reshape the world, inside and out.

But we also have so much literature and research about how the brain is plastic and moldable, about how counseling and conversation and the simple, astounding act of being loved by someone in conversation can piece your brain (and your life) back together. As if grace really is a force that changes us.

This literature is worth its weight in gold as it helps us learn how to love our friends, but Jesus did not need to mention a double-blind study on the effects of trauma or shame to teach us how to love. He simply demonstrated it by walking Peter back through a moment, activating his senses and his memory, and then saying the words of love where Peter remembered only words of pain.

Jesus is the master of friendship and the master of gracious conversation.

One of our friends' greatest needs will be important moments of conversation that help lead them out of their pain. These conversations are not easy, but when we have them on purpose, we are imitating Jesus.

Perhaps this conversation happens after a death in the family. Perhaps it happens after a great moral failure. Perhaps it happens in the midst of great doubt. Perhaps it happens in the midst of unbearable pain. Perhaps you find your friend in the crisis of mental illness. Perhaps you find them in the more normal numbing confusion of how to live well. Whatever the circumstances, when you devote an evening, or a getaway, to finding your friends and using gentle, patient, prolonged, and grace-filled conversation to pull them out of their trauma and into the grip of a loving friend—you are Christ to them in that moment.

> FRIENDS ARE CALLED TO PUNCTUATE LIFE WITH COURAGEOUS CONVERSATIONS.

You are the presence of Jesus beside the fire, you are the words of Jesus reinstating Peter, you are the graciousness of God reminding a friend that they are not stuck in the pain of what has happened; they are called forward, like Peter, through pain and failure, into a life of love.

Friends are called to punctuate life with courageous conversations.

Say Intentional Words

One more thing we can learn from the Master on how to create memories in friendship: say what needs to be said, even when it's awkward.

Recall that one of the things we've learned from modern psychology is that we tend to remember the end of an experience more than anything else.[10] Jesus, again, didn't need to be told. In his final days, he pulled his disciples aside and had the conversation that needed to be had on purpose.

---

10. Heath and Heath, *Power of Moments*, 8–9, 35.

So much of our feelings about our loved ones passes silently through our heads, unspoken and unheard. To say those things out loud is, unsurprisingly, one of the greatest gifts we can give.

Sometimes, like Jesus in John 21 or like we talked about in chapter 2 on honesty, this may be a word with a bit of challenge or rebuke. Remember, Jesus reminded Peter of his betrayal before he reinstated him, and that was on purpose. The wounds of a friend are loving, and sometimes the important words to say are, "I see you making a mistake. And I love you too much not to say it out loud." Say these intentional words. Be the friend who is brave enough to be honest. After all, "only people prepared to lose friends will prove good friends."[11]

On the other hand, sometimes this needs to be intentional words of encouragement that will—if simply spoken—alter the course of someone's life. It may be as simple as, "I don't want to leave this conversation without saying this out loud: I appreciate your friendship so much." Sometimes it may be just naming someone's qualities. Sometimes it's pausing, holding someone by the shoulders, and saying, "I love you," or, "I'm proud of you."

Some may think it strange, but my closest friends and I make it a point to end our calls and more personal hangouts with "I love you." We may add, "I love you, brother," or, "I love you, man," to soften our own awkwardness. But most important things in life are a little bit awkward. That is okay.

That reminder hanging awkwardly in the air—that we love our friends—is worth it. Because we do. And why let it go unsaid? Words call us forward, and they remind us backward. We need to say them on purpose.

11. James Mumford, "Find Brutal Friends," *Comment*, July 7, 2022, comment.org/find -brutal-friends/.

Say things you mean, even when they're awkward and you have to repeat them. Don't let the wonder of it all go unsaid.

The Extraordinary Awaiting in the Ordinary

Cabin weekends and campfires and getaways and late-night conversations go a long way to creating moments, but we don't need extraordinary acts to create extraordinary moments. They come just by being brave enough to use your words and moments on purpose.

I mentioned earlier that I don't remember 90 percent of the meals I've eaten, but on the other hand, I do remember my dinner tables. The place of my ordinary sustenance. I don't remember 90 percent of the conversations I've had with friends, but I do remember my front porch, that cabin outside Front Royal we always went to, that spot on the river, and that kitchen in our college house. I remember these places that have grown rich with the memories of friendship. And that is a grace that sustains. So my advice is this: don't wait for the memories to come. Make them on purpose.

CHAPTER 10

Worship

The Art of Worship and the Habits
of Communal Spiritual Disciplines

It was 6:00 a.m. when I got the call.

One of our friends, who was traveling for work, was trapped in a hotel room in Mali. You may remember this tragic headline from 2015. Terrorists had overtaken the hotel, shot the guards, and were walking the hallways, trying the knobs and murdering defenseless residents.

Absent a miracle, it was only a matter of time for our friend. The internet in his room had remained on, so he had been able to shoot off an email to his loved ones, asking for prayer and a miracle.

One of my friends who saw the email first called me crying, telling me to pray.

I remember getting up in the quiet dark, walking downstairs, lying face down on the floor of my living room, and pleading with the Lord for my friend's life.

While I was doing that, some of our friends had gathered at his parents' house to pray. And then to wait. And then to pray and wait some more.

I later learned that while we were kneeling on floors to pray, he was also kneeling on a floor, leaning against a barricade of furniture he had built and pushing back as he felt a gunman try the knob.

Friendship, I have argued since the first page of this book, is a matter of life and death.

We were made for people, and when we live close to them, we flourish. When we let ourselves drift along the invisible current into loneliness, a real part of us begins to wither, and eventually, it dies. The enemy knows this. Which is why loneliness is not just dangerous, it's evil.

It doesn't do us any good to mince words and avoid the sense of strangeness that talking about evil brings. If we believe in God, then we believe what he says about the world, and what he says is that the world is not just about us and him, but there are other forces in the world that want to tear us apart. Evil is not just real. It is alive. It is active. And it is prowling around every day of our lives, trying all the doorknobs.

I am sure you know this, though you may not care to admit it. And that is understandable. But we do ourselves no favors not to name the reality: evil threatens to tear us apart.

Think about your friends. The ones who you know are addicted to alcohol. Or the ones who you know are suffocating themselves by not opening up. Think about the depression and anxiety that person struggles with that you can't seem to understand. Think about the self-loathing and shame that friend cannot seem to kick. Think about the daddy issues that plague them. Think about the pornography addictions that are going unaddressed. Think, for a moment, about all this darkness that rages in each of our everyday lives.

The Bible is fairly blunt about this. "Your enemy the devil prowls around like a roaring lion looking for someone to devour."[1] That may sound like superstition to the modern world. But to the Christian with open eyes, that sounds exactly like the world we live in.

None of us live in peacetime. No matter what it may seem like when we drive the streets to work, sit down to coffee with a friend, or hold the hands of our children on the walk to school. It may be a sunny day. But we are at war.

However, the war analogy goes only so far. Our enemy is not nearly so much like a unified nation overseas full of people who want to take over and rule us. Our enemy is much more like a terrorist, one who moves in and out of our midst without being noticed and then all at once wants to invade the normal places of our peace and kill everything that moves. Normally he does this by whispering a homemade bomb of a lie into our ears. Normally he speaks in a voice that sounds suspiciously like our own thoughts. Often, we don't realize it at all.

FRIENDS ARE ESSENTIAL IN THE BATTLE AGAINST EVIL.

That is the reality we live in.

When I think about my friend kneeling against his barricade with evil on the other side of the door, I think about the reality of that fight. Physically and spiritually. It brings the Cain story back to mind: evil is crouching at the door.

Waking up to the reality of evil is a shock. So is waking up to a phone call at 6:00 a.m. telling you that your friend is about to be murdered.

This is not the way we want the world to be. But, unfortunately, it is the reality. The alarm bells are ringing, and the

---

1. 1 Peter 5:8.

question is, What real friend would ignore them? What real friend would not take that 6:00 a.m. call?

Not a one. A covenant friend wakes up, gets on the ground, and fights with you. Fights for you. Friends are essential in the battle against evil.

The Art of Worship as an Act of Resistance

It is as encouraging as it is astounding that whenever we read about evil in the Bible, the idea of fear is not even close to being the main theme. In fact, the idea of fear is far more associated with encounters with holiness—"Do not be afraid" is usually the refrain of the angels, not the demons.

Rather, when the Bible talks about evil, it talks about worship.

Peter, in talking about the lion of the devil, calls us to stand firm in faith.[2] Paul in Ephesians calls us to stand against the devil and darkness by truth, by the Word of God, and by clinging to the gospel.[3] The psalmist writes "I will fear no evil"[4] because he knows the character of God, the shepherd who, with a rod and staff, tends the sheep, and that is the psalmist's comfort.

The courage to fight evil actually begins with the courage to worship.

And how do we do this but together? As Peter goes on to write, "Resist him and be firm in the faith, because you know that your brothers throughout the world are undergoing the same kinds of suffering."[5]

---

2. 1 Peter 5:8.
3. Ephesians 6:10–20.
4. Psalm 23:4.
5. 1 Peter 5:9 (ISV).

Friends don't abandon one another in times of need, they fight for one another. But the weapon is worship. Evil is crouching at the door, which means that friendship is not real, not full, not covenantal, not true spiritual friendship—until it is full of worship.

The stakes are high, but the call is clear. Our friendships must be full of worship.

Friendship as Worship

Before we talk about how worship can be a part of friendship, it is important to remember that the act of friendship in and of itself *is* a real act of worship.

Recall the Genesis story and how we were made for friendship. Simply being in friendship with someone else means we are imitating the Trinity, which is inherently an act of worship.

This means that to be happy in the presence of a friend is like a song, a prayer, a sacrifice, a stick of incense. We feel the pleasure of God when we practice friendship because it is an act of worship to him, and there is nothing second to feeling the pleasure of God. It is an unparalleled power in our lives.

Often, we may think that friends need to "do something that seems Christian" to validate our friendship as an act of worship. As if we need to be friends and then pray together, or go to small group, or sing some worship songs to make our friendship an act of worship to God. These things are wonderful, but our friendships stand as acts of worship far before we even get to those other things.

Friendship itself is the main act of worship. God sees your friends. He sees you too. He sees your work in relationships, and he loves it! He rejoices in it and in you. He is pleased when you act like a friend because you are acting like Christ, and that is the image he made you in and the image he is redeeming you in.

The opposite is also true. When you're so busy getting your family right, doing well at your job, being present for your kids, serving your spouse, and making it to the Sunday evening service and the Wednesday night small group too, there can still be a gaping hole in your worship.

It is totally possible to live the picture-perfect nuclear family and church life and still have a gaping hole in your heart because, when it comes down to it, you are living that life friendless and alone. You are not vulnerable to your spouse, no one in your small group really knows you because you don't share, and you don't have real friends because work and the kids take up all your time.

I believe we should look at this kind of life the way we look at the lives of functioning alcoholics or chain smokers. You can do a lot of other things right, but if this is how you're living, you're still on a path of death and destruction. It's just a matter of time until you implode.

Likewise, when we live without friendship, we are missing a key area of worship to God. And worship is a matter of life and death.

This is why having vulnerable friendships in your life is probably the best spiritual medicine for anxiety or depression. This is why a counselor would prescribe vulnerable friendships if it were that simple; all the data shows that lifelong friendships are the greatest predictor of health.[6]

---

6. Robert Waldinger and Marc Schulz, "The Lifelong Power of Close Relationships," *Wall Street Journal*, January 13, 2023, www.wsj.com/articles/the-lifelong-power-of -close-relationships-11673625450.

Worship breeds health, and friendship is worship.

This is why it is hard for deep, dark secrets to exist for very long when vulnerable friendship enters the picture. Sin "wants us alone,"[7] but friendship declares war on such isolation.

Fighting for covenant friendship means, by definition, you are fighting the evil that prowls. We begin to do that by practicing friendship.

SIN "WANTS US ALONE," BUT FRIENDSHIP DECLARES WAR ON SUCH ISOLATION.

But we do not end there.

Friendship by itself may be worship, but worship spurs worship, and those who are seeking after the covenant friendship of Christ will find the spiritual disciplines of Scripture and prayer indispensable tools in the fight for friendship.

Habits of Scripture in Friendship

"Thank you for sharing. Christ loves you unconditionally."

As you will recall, these are the words my friend and I often end our accountability exchanges with.

Of course, such words are found in Scripture, and I could easily go read them on my own. I could flip to Jeremiah 31:3 and read that God loves me with "an everlasting love" and that he draws me in with "unfailing kindness."

Why, then, do I need a friend to say them?

Why does it feel like such a benediction when my brother, after hearing all the ways I am flawed, says, "God loves you, and so do I"?

---

7. Dietrich Bonhoeffer, *Life Together: The Classic Exploration of Christian Community*, trans. John W. Doberstein (New York: HarperSanFrancisco, 1978), 111.

Because the word of Christ is truer in the mouth of a friend.[8]

Speaking the words of Scripture to your friends is an altogether unique power.

Of course, they "know" them. But if knowing Scripture was all we needed, then we'd all be saints. The fact is we need to feel Scripture, hear Scripture, and experience Scripture over and over and over. That is what friends are for.

> THE WORD OF CHRIST IS TRUER IN THE MOUTH OF A FRIEND.

Keep in mind, I do not mean to suggest that the words of Scripture are magic incantations that we can recite over one another and—poof—we'll be better. Anyone who has grieved, anyone who has been knocked off the horse of life by mental illness, anyone who has truly doubted God—anyone who is a normal human being—knows that someone who ignores listening and spouts off the first Scripture that comes to mind speaks not in the Holy Spirit but in the platitudes of Job's friends.

A friend is first present. A friend knows how to sit in silence. A friend knows how to hug you until you cry. A friend knows how to cry with you before saying anything at all.

But a friend also knows that there comes a time to call your

---

8. Bonhoeffer puts it this way: "God has put this Word into the mouth of men in order that it may be communicated to other men. When one person is struck by the Word, he speaks it to others. God has willed that we should seek and find His living Word in the witness of a brother, in the mouth of man. Therefore, the Christian needs another Christian who speaks God's Word to him. He needs him again and again when he becomes uncertain and discouraged, for by himself he cannot help himself without belying the truth. He needs his brother as a bearer and proclaimer of the divine word of salvation. He needs his brother solely because of Jesus Christ. The Christ in his own heart is weaker than the Christ in the word of his brother; his own heart is uncertain, his brother's is sure." (*Life Together*, 22–23.)

friend forward. A friend knows that they bear a responsibility to speak the word of Christ that is stronger in their mouth. It is a holy obligation. There are many ways to do this. The table on the next page describes a few ideas.

I remember once my dear friend and fellow missionary in China, Katie, was sitting at a table with my wife and me for dinner. I cannot remember what had gotten her down, but she was sad and asked, "Would you share the gospel with me?"

As all important moments with friends are, it was an awkward request.

"Sharing the gospel" was what we normally did with Chinese students. But she just kept looking at me, waiting for me to answer her question.

Not knowing exactly what to do, I began telling a story. A story about an all-powerful, loving being who created the world. A triune God who loved all things into existence. A story about people who—though they were made for the love of God—wandered off, looking to be loved by other things. A story about all the havoc and evil and suffering that brought— and how human history is a story of that awful suffering. How we could still feel it now at that table where I went on babbling. But I also told her a story about a God who altered history by coming into it. A God who took on human form and a name— Jesus. A God-man named Jesus who lived and loved and died and rose again to break the back of death and sin and suffering. A God who sent his Holy Spirit and said that those who believe in him and call on his name are his kids. They're children of the King. And the King is coming back. That's what we're waiting for: the day when the King will come and take away all this sin and suffering and death once and for all.

Ways to Interweave Scripture into Friendships

COMMON READING PLANS

At times I've read through devotionals with friends so that the morning themes can come up in conversation. In certain seasons of the church calendar, our congregation will do the same. Currently many of my friends read from the Book of Common Prayer both because it helps make a habit of Scripture reading and because it gives us a common reading that can be discussed.

THEMATIC VERSES

For a long time I had an email chain with friends where the automatic signature block was a paraphrase of Psalm 133, "How good and pleasant when brothers dwell together in unity." Now I have a text chain with Steve and Matt titled "Three Strands" (Eccl. 4:12). Both of these serve as reminders that Scripture is the heartbeat and foundation of our friendships.

GROUP DEVOTIONS

Attending the same Bible study may seem obvious. If you are in a small group with friends, then diving into the Scriptures together can and should be normal. However, the reality for me is that I'm not in a small group with most of my friends. So Scripture has to be intentionally brought in. While our cabin weekends are few and far between in this season, when we do have one there will be some time of prayer and Scripture reading that helps call us to center.

TEXTING SCRIPTURE

My friend Drew is so good at texting out a Scripture he may be praying for you. My friends and I also have a text chain (the one I mentioned earlier) where prayer requests and verses are shared. This helps make it easy and normal to punctuate our ongoing conversation with occasional metions of Scriptures that have moved us. It gives us a place to put this special kind of conversation.

So on that night, at that dinner, I told her, we had something to hope for. And tomorrow, we had something to work for.

And that was it. We were all a bit bleary eyed remembering the good news together. But I'll never forget the little act of courage she showed by asking her friend to retell her the good news. I'll never forget how her request reminded me that that's what friends are for.

We retell the good story to one another when we need it. That's one way we get on our knees together and fight for communal faith in a world that wants us alone.

Habits of Prayer in Friendship

There is an awesome power we carry, as friends, to lift one another up in prayer. But the reality is that most of this prayer we do for one another will not come in predawn hours on our knees. That kind of prayer is wonderful. But most of us will pray in much more ordinary moments. That, too, is an extraordinary thing, to have friends who knit one another together in an ongoing network of ordinary moments of prayer.

Each night, Lauren and I kneel together beside our bed to pray before turning out the lights. Even when we're mad at each other or exhausted from the day or anything else you can be on a normal night of marriage. Sometimes we're too tired and we lie down and reach out for the other's hand, but not a night goes by that we don't say a short prayer together. And often, it has the name of a friend in it. A friend who miscarried, a friend who's sick, a friend who's sad, a friend whose parent is slowly dying, a friend who wishes for marriage, a friend who wishes for a happier marriage, a friend who suffers in the wake of divorce, a

BECOMING MORE LIKE JESUS NECESSARILY MEANS BECOMING MORE LIKE A FRIEND.

friend who wants more friends, or a friend who longs for more faith. We pray for those friends, however briefly, before we sleep. Because otherwise, the reality is that we would tell people "I will pray for you" without ever making time to do it.

I don't believe the logic of the world that says those tiny, tired, and wishful moments have nothing to with the weight of the world's reality, which turns unceasingly toward suffering and chaos. I reject it, one prayer at a time every night, with the logic of faith. That prayer moves mountains. Mountains of doubt, mountains of pain, mountains of suffering, and mountains of isolation that keep my friends from the life with God they were made for.

We fight for that because our friends need us. And they fight for us too.

I woke up to a text one morning from a dear friend who wrote, "Prayed for your book this morning. Finish strong." I needed that. Writing drains me like nothing I have ever known.

But that's not all. If I search my text messages for the word "prayer," the results are joyfully uncountable. Even the smartphone gets stuck logging them all. Because in real ways our constant communication as friends is an endless network of "pray for me" and "pray for you," a holy chatter between the triune dance we've been invited into, of one friend, another friend, and God himself in the middle.

My friends tend to make a habit of trying not to say, "I will pray for you." Instead, we say, "I just prayed for you." It's a small act to make sure that the web of requests and confessions is not the hollow echo of a life of prayer that we never get to but the holy echo of prayers that are nearly unceasing—in real time and for real people.

Recently I caught up with a dear friend at the gym after a workout, and we got to talking about our kids and school. She began (I think not realizing it) sharing anxieties with me about her son and his teachers. I honestly needed to hurry up and get to work, but I could tell this was important to her, so I reminded myself that this was a time I needed to serve a friend by listening and that work would be fine if I got there fifteen minutes later than I had planned.

Afterward she texted me apologizing, saying that she should have just gone and prayed about it. I immediately texted back sharing with her that I rarely know what to pray for until I talk to a friend, so I'm glad she spent time processing. Sometimes, the gift of friends is not that they pray for us but that through them we realize what we need to pray for.

A couple of chapters back I mentioned that some friends and I texted about praying for a friend's career decision. Well after the prayer was done and the decision was made, one of my friends texted this: "I have really enjoyed praying for this and you. I have a hard time knowing what I need to pray for myself and praying for someone else's specific need is really helpful in pinpointing my own."

I resonate so much with this friend and my friend at the gym. It is in conversation with friends that I often get led to prayer and then back and forth all over again.

I applaud the hour-long devotion in the morning where you pray for a list of all the people in your life. I really do. But I also lift up the ordinary believer, like you and me, who finds this holy act of worship in the ordinary and "unceasing" small prayers that change lives.

Habits to Interweave Prayer into Friendships

TEXT CHAINS

I recommend passing prayer requests as often as possible on whatever regular communication chains you have—email, social media apps, texts, or otherwise. I even suggest having a chain dedicated to prayer requests so anyone can feel like they can send something anytime. I also heartily endorse my friends' habit of saying "Just prayed for you" instead of "I will pray for you" as a way to let prayer interrupt your day.

NOTEBOOKS

I have at times kept a notebook of prayer requests for friends. While I don't have one now, I enjoy going back and reading years later what I was praying about for them. I did this the other day, and it was a remarkable moment to praise God for the requests that were answered.

EMERGENCY MEETINGS

In occasional moments of crisis, my friends and I have called gatherings at one another's houses to pray about someone or something. These are very difficult moments, usually marked with darkness and suffering, but in my memory they become very dear moments. As I look back, they seem like real evidence of Psalm 23. That though we have walked through the valley of the shadow of death, he has been with us, particularly as we have gathered for prayer.

BENEDICTIONS

It is not unusual that after a meaningful or deep or vulnerable evening of conversation with my friends, someone will suggest we close in prayer. I so appreciate this as a norm. Usually we need the benediction of prayer to send us on from conversations like that, and making it a norm is one small way to punctuate your friendships with prayer. Be brave (and awkward) enough to offer to be the one to close a conversation in prayer.

*(**continued**)*

───────────── CHRISTMAS CARDS ─────────────

Recently my wife, Lauren, suggested that we keep all the Christmas cards people send us next to our family Bible. On family devotion nights the kids pick someone out of the stack and pray for them during the week. This has been a special way to turn the annual notes passed back and forth into a recurring rhythm of intentional prayer for other families.

───────────── BEDTIME PRAYERS ─────────────

I cannot recommend enough the habit of short, bedside prayers. Often it is in the evening when the weight of the day hits me. It is then that I remember the difficult news I may have heard. It is good, then, to close the day reminding ourselves that we and our friends rest in God's hands and not our own. Make a habit of kneeling by your bed to pray for rest and for friends, and it just may become a lifetime habit of prayer.

Our Names Are Written on His Hands

That morning at six o'clock, we prayed on our knees while my friend in Mali knelt on his knees against a door, feeling a gunman try the knob.

But when my friend finally opened his door, it was not to a gunman but to a burly Frenchman. He was a first responder on the special ops team. The way our friend tells it is that the Frenchman said, "Grab my arm, and do not let go." And guns raised, they escaped down a flight of stairs.

It would be almost a week later before we got to see our friend again. Thankfully, the US Embassy that intervened to fly the escaped Americans home did a bit of counseling to help everyone at least begin to deal with the trauma of having survived a terrorist attack.

But when my friend did get back home, you wouldn't believe the party we threw.

I'll never forget it. It was right before Thanksgiving, when—providentially—many happened to be back in town. Everyone gathered at my house, and in the living room for a long evening we gave thanks, we sang hymns, we read Scripture to one another, we prayed, we wept, and then we sang and read and prayed some more.

Then we poured drinks and stood by a backyard fire and talked the night away.

The walls echoed with worship that night. But it would be a mistake to think that was just because we prayed and sang—the walls echoed with worship because they surrounded friends who were real friends, who in this instance and many others, literally and metaphorically, knelt on the ground together.

THE POWER OF GOD IN COMMUNITY IS NOT IN OUR FRIENDSHIPS THEMSELVES BUT IN THE WAY THEY ECHO AND REFLECT THE TRUEST FRIENDSHIP: THE FRIENDSHIP OF GOD HIMSELF.

The stakes of life are high. That night will forever remind me that covenant friendship is a matter of life and death.

I saw something unmistakably supper-of-the-Lamb like that night: the gathering of believers, when the world is made right and we come together with everyone we have ever loved, before the presence of God, to party.

That evening, I was reminded that the power of God in community is not in our friendships themselves but in the way they echo and reflect the truest friendship: the friendship of God himself.

We need one another in the fight against evil—that much is certain. But we can't save one another. Not in the end.

But there is a Friend who can save us.

That night, when we gathered to pray, my friend told me another story he heard from the hotel that day, from a fellow American he met at the counseling debriefings afterward. The American told them that she had been pulled out by a US marine.

She said that, like the Frenchman who saved my friend, the marine's instruction was "Hold my hand, and don't let go." But when she looked down at the marine's arm, she saw that on his forearm, written in thick, black marker, were the numbers of different hotel rooms with Xs through them. She realized they were the room numbers of the Americans in the hotel. Each time he pulled someone out of a room, the room got crossed off and he went to find the next American.

This I will ever hold as an image of covenant friendship. That we know one another's names. We know where our friends are. And we will come to find one another. Because we imitate the God who does just that.

In Isaiah we are told that there is another man with our names written on him.[9] And in Revelation we are told he is coming back for us. That man is stronger than any marine. There is no evil—not even death—that can hold him. His name is Jesus.

He is the one who has called us by name, reaching through the current of death to grab us, hold us fast, and raise us to life.

---

9. "See, I have engraved you on the palms of my hands" (Isa. 49:16).

Jesus is the strong man who laid down his own life, and rose again, so that he could say to us "I have called you friends."

Receive the covenant friendship of that man. Then turn and give it to the world. It is a matter of life and death.

EPILOGUE

The Fire of Friendship

Last night when I should have been picking up the house or working on one of the million work deadlines I'm behind on, I instead sat with two of my closest friends, Steve and Matt, over a fire on my back porch. We did what we always do. We spoke honestly and told our secrets.

Look at it one way, and it was a normal Tuesday night chatting over a firepit. We talked of work stress and fighting mental illness, of workouts and difficulties in our marriages. We shared about children and talked politics. There was a lot of laughing (and actually some crying too). But for just an hour and a half or so, between kids' bedtimes and getting ready for more work the next day, we found some conversation.

So look at it another way, and it was a phenomenally countercultural act in a world of loneliness. In a time when we could have scrolled phones, worked more, or not worried about driving anywhere and just sent text updates instead, we sat with our bodies in the same place and told things we didn't have to tell.

When you write a book about friendship, you think in ideas like vulnerability and covenant, like forgiveness and geography. And I really do hope those concepts help you. But when you live out friendship, those ideas inevitably melt down into moments like last night. Where in a simple yet radical act, it all happens at once and you come together over a fire and live one more day as a person without secrets who can practice being fully known and fully loved by Jesus and by others.

These radically ordinary nights change everything.

One of the small pleasures of last night was that before Steve and Matt came over, I asked my two older boys, Whit and Asher (who are eleven and eight), to start the fire for us. Lauren was at a church meeting; they worked diligently, thrilled to be asked to play with fire, as I got my other two younger sons down to bed.

By the time I finished everything, my two friends were sitting at the fire with my two older boys, chatting. I let them sit for the first few minutes of our conversation before sending them off to bed too.

I cherish those moments of letting them watch friendship. I want them to grow up seeing what covenant friendship looks like, because I really do believe friendship will save the world.

Friendship will save the world because that is what God, the redeemer of all things, is doing in the world. He is making us friends and sending us out to call the world into that relationship.

As I wrote in chapter 5, we live in a moment when it is incredibly difficult to meaningfully share your faith in words. Our neighbors have an almost entirely different understanding of what words like love, justice, faith, and sacrifice mean. And that is very painful. If you are like me, you increasingly feel like you are on the margin of a world happening around you, one that doesn't understand you and that you don't know how to speak to anymore. Like a child in a dysfunctional family, you just watch everyone yell and long so badly for something different.

And yet it is in this very time that I feel ever more strongly about what I just wrote: that friendship will save the world.

Madeleine L'Engle once wisely wrote that "we draw people to Christ not by loudly discrediting what they believe, by telling them how wrong they are and how right we are, but by showing them a light that is so lovely that they want with all their hearts to know the source of it."[1]

When I ask my boys to start a fire and sit with my friends for a moment, what I'm actually doing is inviting them to gaze on such "a light so lovely." When we kindle the fire of friendship in a world of lonely hostility, we raise a beautiful light in the darkness. We say, "Yes, relationships are messy and full of pain, but Jesus knew us fully and loved us anyway, so we will do the same." Nearly all the people I have seen come to know (or come back to know) Jesus have done so because of being invited into circles of Christian friendship, in being invited to come sit beside the fire.

What would it look like in your life to build such a fire?

In a cultural winter of loneliness, what if we Christians were the ones building those fires? What if we invited all the travelers on the lonely road of modern life to stop by and, even if we don't speak their language, to come over and warm themselves by the fire? I think that would be a light to the world.

You are made for people. And that means you need friendship to walk with God the way you were made to. But your neighbors were made for people too. And we just might be living in a time when friendship is the primary way those neighbors will come to know the Jesus that they were made for.

This call to covenant friendship, then, is not just for you. It's for your children, your neighbors, and the world that God made for people.

Build the fire of friendship. Pass the torch. And raise it high. May it be a light so lovely.

---

1. Madeleine L'Engle, *Herself: Reflections on a Writing Life*.

Acknowledgments

You can wake to watch the sunrise, but anyone who does knows they have nothing to do with it. They've only arranged their life to witness the miracle of it.

So you can arrange your life for friendship. But when it happens, it remains a miracle. Like the sunrise, friendship is not something you accomplish so much as something you arrange your life for, bear witness to, and then give thanks for. Here, then, are my thanks:

I have joked that my first two books came out of crisis. And it's true. But this book is different. It has come forth from blessing. I stand on the shoulders of you, my friends, and from here I get to watch the sunrise of these friendships we share. What a miracle it all is. I have no idea who I would have become without you, but I'm so grateful for who we have become together. Because of you, I am confident. Which is no small thing. Confident that whatever the future holds, we will walk through it together.

I dare not name any names here. I wouldn't even know where to start with the ordering, and I'm horrified at the thought of forgetting someone and diminishing the gifts we have shared.

So instead I nod my head to all of you: from the evenings of Sycamore youth group and the afternoons at Midlothian High School, from the long days at University of Virginia and the short summers in San Diego, from the nights in Shanghai and the dinners and drinks in Washington, D.C., and maybe most of all, to all of you rooting here in the rich soils of Richmond, Virginia. May we grow something beautiful.

I lift my hands and thank God for each of you. And even more, I look forward to all the days still to come.

Appendix

Friendship Covenant

As I mentioned in chapter 4 on covenant, this is a covenant my friends and I wrote. Though it has never been signed, our discussion of it was formative. I give it here so that others might be able to make some use of it. Perhaps it will call you forward to commit. Perhaps you will even sign it.

A Commitment to Covenant Friendship

Purpose: This is a statement of what we believe and what we aspire to be. We articulate it so that we can better understand the commitment, hold one another to the commitment, and invite others into the same character of commitment—with us, but also with others who do not know us. We see it as an umbrella under which many, many friends can sit. But we see it as only a beginning. Every set of friends must make their friendships specific. This calls for more conversation, not less. We believe this kind of commitment happens in and among other commitments—such as to marriages, churches, and families. We believe this kind of covenant strengthens all of them.

1. The purpose of friendship is for the glory of, and to make us more like, the Father, Son, and Holy Spirit. We imitate and exalt the triune God.
2. We were created for friendships and are most human when in them. But as created beings with limited

capacities, time, and abilities—we can be in only so many friendships.

3. We have a multiplicity of commitments, but we exist outside the economics of scarcity. Time is a limited resource, but love is exponential. Faithful living demands a balance of time, commitments, and priorities, but we do not fear running out of love.

4. Our friendships are interwoven within the foundations of the church, marriages, and families. Friendships not only strengthen these institutions but also are essential to them. We exist outside of market competition. We resist jealousy.

5. The structure of friendships is such that multiple people are pointed at the same goal. In drawing toward the goal, friends draw closer together. Thus friendships are not constrained by spatial dimensions—we can be outward and inward at the same time. We are healthiest when we are.

6. Being left out of friendships is painful. We commit to protecting others from this and repenting when we are the cause of it.

7. Covenantal friendships mean that we commit to pursuing our friends, even when they leave us. Covenantal friendships mean that when we falter and leave them, we expect and hope our friends will pursue us.

8. We commit our words to one another. We commit to being generous in our encouragements and specific in our rebukes.

9. We believe in the reciprocity of belief and practice. **Our friendships are predicated on shared beliefs, but they are** given life by our shared daily practices. Neither comes first, each feeds the other, and neither can fully exist without the other.

10. Our friendships must be as much for the good of those not in them as for the ones in them. When we are insular, we are failing. Specifically, in service to the poor, disenfranchised, downtrodden, and oppressed, we become better friends. Our friendships need to serve others.

11. Our friendships are hard and are characterized more by struggle than success.

12. We acknowledge that location deeply shapes friendships, but friendships still span locations.

13. We submit our financial decisions to the definitions of our friendships, not the opposite.

14. In contemporary America, houses, careers, and finances are some of the fundamental determinants of the possibility of friendships. However, we commit to giving friendships priority and letting the cast of friendship shape our homes, our careers, our finances, and everything that comes from them.

15. We believe friendships are powerful in the kingdom of God. And that true friendships across families, churches, neighborhoods, countries, languages, and causes can bring about the kingdom of God in uniquely powerful ways.

Habits of the Household

Practicing the Story of God in Everyday Family Rhythms

Justin Whitmel Earley

Discover simple habits and easy-to-implement daily rhythms that will help you find meaning beyond the chaos of family life as you create a home where kids and parents alike practice how to love God and each other.

You long for tender moments with your children, but do you ever find yourself too busy to stop, make eye contact, and say something you really mean? Daily habits are powerful ways to shape the heart, but do you find yourself giving in to screen time just to get through the day? You want to parent with purpose, but do you know how to start?

Award-winning author and father of four Justin Whitmel Earley understands the tension between how you long to parent and what your daily life actually looks like. In this bestseller *Habits of the Household*, Earley gives you the tools you need to create structure—from mealtimes to bedtimes—that free you to parent toddlers, kids, and teens with purpose. Learn how to:

- Develop a bedtime liturgy to settle your little ones and ground them in God's love
- Discover a new framework for discipline as discipleship
- Acquire simple practices for more regular and meaningful family mealtimes
- Open your eyes to the spirituality of parenting, seeing small moments as big opportunities for spiritual formation
- Develop a custom age chart for your family to plan your shared years under the same roof

Each chapter in *Habits of the Household* ends with practical patterns, prayers, or liturgies that your family can put into practice right away. As you create liberating rhythms around your everyday routines, you will find your family has a greater sense of peace and purpose as your home becomes a place where, above all, you learn how to love.

Available in stores and online!

From the Publisher

GREAT BOOKS

ARE EVEN BETTER WHEN THEY'RE SHARED!

Help other readers find this one:

- Post a review at your favorite online bookseller

- Post a picture on a social media account and share why you enjoyed it

- Send a note to a friend who would also love it—or better yet, give them a copy

Thanks for reading!